The

AIFMD

Quick Guide

(Basic concept and the rules)

Table of Contents

1.0)   **Introduction:** --- **9**

1.1)   Purpose of this book: --------------------------------------9

1.2)   Scope, contents and implementation time table: ------ 10

1.3)   The position of Directives in EU Law: ----------------- 11

1.4)   The AIFMD Implementation Regulation: ------------- 12

1.5)   The position of Regulations in EU law: ---------------- 13

1.6)   Other documents building the AIFMD framework:-- 14

1.7)   National interpretation: --------------------------------- 14

1.8)   Consequences of not implementing the rules: -------- 15

1.9)   Funds potentially captured by the AIF definition:---- 17

2.0)   **Capital requirements:** --------------------------------- **18**

2.1)   Capital types to be provided:---------------------------- 19

2.2)   Initial own funds and internally managed AIFs: ------ 21

2.3)   Exception for Super-ManCos: -------------------------- 21

2.4)   Insurance coverage instead of additional own funds for
          liability risk: -- 22

2.5)   Definition and management of own funds: ------------ 22

3.0)   **Delegation:** -- **24**

3.1)   Introduction to delegation: ----------------------------- 25

3.2)   General delegation requirements: ---------------------- 26

3.2.1)   Letter box entity: --- 26

3.2.2)   Objective reasons for delegation: ---------------------- 27

3.2.3)   access of the delegate to global trading capabilities.- 27

3.2.3)   Ultimate responsibility of the AIFM:------------------ 27

3.3)   Contract with the delegate: ----------------------------- 29

3.4)   Vendor due diligence: -----------------------------------30

3.4.1)   Vendor skills and reputation check: ---------------------30

3.4.2)   Potential prevention of effective supervision: ---------30

3.4.3)   Delegation of risk and portfolio management: --------31

3.4.4)   Conflicts of interest assessment: -------------------------33

3.5)   Sub-delegation: --34

4.0)   Valuations: -- 35

4.1)   Who can act as a valuer: ----------------------------------36

4.2)   Minimum frequency requirements: ----------------------37

4.3)   Valuation policies and procedures: ----------------------37

4.4)   Other valuation-related requirements: ------------------38

5.0)   Organisational requirements: ----------------------- 40

5.1)   Conflicts of interest: --------------------------------------41

5.1.1)   Organisational precautions: -------------------------------41

5.1.2)   Conflicts of interest policy: -------------------------------42

5.1.3)   Identification of conflicts of interests: ------------------42

5.1.4)   Conflicts of interest disclosures: -----------------------43

5.2)   Rules on establishing AIFM functions: -----------------44

5.2.1)   Separation requirements: ---------------------------------44

5.2.2)   Set-up of independent control functions: ---------------45

5.3)   Minimum company infrastructure and transaction
         processing requirements: ---------------------------------47

5.3.1)   Data security, business continuity and documentation
         of company structure: -------------------------------------47

5.3.2)   Using prime brokers, order aggregation, corporate
         actions: --48

5.4)   Remuneration: -- 50

5.4.1)   Remuneration requirements of Annex II, AIFMD: -- 50

5.4.2)   Remuneration and Commission Recommendation
           2009/384/EC: --- 57

5.4.3)   ESMA Guidance on sound remuneration for AIFMs: 58

5.5)   Fair treatment of investors: ------------------------------ 63

5.5.1)   Payment of fees, commissions and other benefits: --- 63

5.5.2)   Best execution: -- 64

6.0)   Authorisation: -- 67

6.1)   Lighter regime: -- 68

6.1.1)   Conditions for using the lighter regime: --------------- 68

6.1.2)   Information to be provided to Competent Authorities: -
           -- 69

6.1.3)   Opting in: -- 70

6.2)   Regular authorisation: ----------------------------------- 71

6.2.1)   Authorisation of EU AIFMs: ---------------------------- 71

6.2.2)   Authorisation of non-EU AIFMs: ----------------------- 72

6.3)   The Member State of Reference assessment: --------- 77

6.3.1)   AIFMD rules on the MoR selection (Directive
           2011/61/EU): --- 77

6.3.2)   Change of marketing strategy: -------------------------- 80

6.3.3)   The rules of Commission Implementing Directive
           448/2013: --- 80

7.0)   Passporting regime: ----------------------------------- 85

7.1)   Introduction to passporting: ---------------------------- 86

7.2)   Passporting for EU AIFMs: ----------------------------- 88

7.2.1)   Passporting for EU AIFs: ---------------------------------88

7.2.1.1)   Passport for managing AIFs established in another
           Member State:--88

7.2.1.2)   Passport for marketing in the AIFM's Home Member
           State: 88

7.2.1.3)   Passporting for marketing in other Member States: --90

7.2.2)   Passporting for non-EU AIFs:----------------------------90

7.2.2.1)   Passport for managing non-EU AIFs:--------------------90

7.2.2.2)   Passport for marketing non-EU AIFs in the Union: --91

7.3)   Passporting for non-EU AIFMs: ------------------------92

7.3.1)   Passporting for EU AIFs: ---------------------------------92

7.3.1.1)   Managing AIFs established in another Member State:--
           --92

7.3.1.2)   Marketing of EU AIFs in the Union:--------------------93

7.3.2)   Passporting for non-EU AIFs:----------------------------94

7.3.2.1)   Marketing of non-EU AIFs in the Union: --------------94

7.4)   Private placement regime: ----------------------------95

8.0)   Appointment of the depositary: ---------------------- 97

8.1)   Entities accepted as a depositary:------------------------98

8.2)   Entities which should not act as a depositary: ------- 100

8.3)   Location of the depositary: ----------------------------- 101

8.4)   Contract with the depositary: --------------------------- 102

9.0)   Risk management: ----------------------------------104

9.1)   Establishing the risk management function: --------- 105

9.2)   Operational risk: --------------------------------------- 107

9.3)   Liquidity risk management:---------------------------- 108

9.4)   Securitisation positions:--------------------------------109

9.5)   Mandatory checks and reviews: ------------------------112

10.0)   Acquiring control over companies: ---------------- 115

10.1)   Notification and disclosure requirements: ------------116

10.2)   Prohibition on capital reductions: ----------------------117

11.0)   Reporting and mandatory documents: ------------ 118

11.1)   Annual report: ---119

11.2)   The prospectus:--122

11.3)   Periodic disclosures to investors:-----------------------124

11.4)   Reporting to competent authorities: -------------------126

12.0)   AIFMD terms and definitions:---------------------- 129

Internally managed AIF---129

Interests of investors---130

Issuer   ---130

Legal representative --131

Leverage   ---131

Managing AIFs ---132

Marketing --132

Master AIF ---132

Member state of reference --132

Non-EU AIF --133

Non-EU-AIFM ---133

Non-listed company --133

Own funds---133

Parent undertaking --134

Prime broker ---134

Professional investor --- 134

Qualifying holding -- 135

Employee representatives --- 135

Retail investor -- 135

Subsidiary--- 136

Supervisory authorities in relation to Non-EU-AIFs ------------ 136

Supervisory authorities in relation to Non-EU-AIFMs---------- 136

Securitisations special purpose entities ---------------------------- 137

UCITS   -- 137

AIF   -- 138

Branch of AIFM -- 138

Carried interest --- 139

Close link --- 139

Competent Authorities--- 140

Feeder AIF--- 143

Financial instrument-- 143

Holding company--- 144

AIF home member state -- 145

AIFM host member state --- 146

Initial capital-- 146

Definition of the term capital commitment----------------------- 147

Relevant person -- 147

Definition of the terms securitisation, securitisation position,

sponsor and tranche --- 148

Definition of loss of a financial instrument held in custody---- 149

Depositary's discharge of liability in case of loss of a financial
instrument --- 151
Objective reasons for the depositary to contract a discharge of
liability --- 154

1.0) Introduction:

1.1) Purpose of this book:

Regulatory change is one of the biggest challenges for banks active in international financial markets. Since the financial crisis of 2008, regulators have tightened the regimes and the cost of ensuring compliance with new rules has increased the cost of doing business. Implementing new regulation is not a one-off exercise, as most frameworks demand that the addressees need to be compliant with defined requirements at any time. So, financial institutions are forced to (i) understand the parts of the regulations which are applicable to them, (ii) identify the legal entities which need to achieve compliance, (iii) initially implement all requirements into day-to-day operational processes and (iv) reassure compliance from time to time.

Often regulations consist of more than a single document. Most EU directives for example are equipped with an Implementation Regulation and various Delegated Regulations developed by the EU Commission. In reality those documents contain a lot of duplication and not all provisions apply to the addressee (e.g. the AIFMD contains many rules for Competent Authorities and ESMA). The pure mass of regulatory text, the language used and the document structure prevents even industry insiders from understanding the content by just reading the documents.

This book intends to filter out all AIFMD provisions applicable to AIFMs and to present them in a digestible form and structure. It might also serve Independent Control Functions within the financial industry like Compliance, Operational Risk Control, Business Risk Management Units and Internal and External Audit Units as a guide for examining post implementation reviews or topic-related analysis.

The structure of this book will allow you to quickly identify your specific topic of interest. Each of the 10 chapters offers you an introduction to the topic, an overview of the applicable provisions and a summary of the most important rules.

1.2)   Scope, contents and implementation time table:

The AIFMD is the Alternative Fund Managers Directive (Directive 2011/61/EU) introduced by the European Union. It covers the management, administration and marketing of alternative investment funds (AIFs) and regulates the Alternative Investment Fund Manager (AIFM) and not the Alternative Investment Fund itself. An AIF is defined as a 'collective investment undertaking' that is not subject to the UCITS regime, and includes hedge funds, private equity funds, real estate funds and others. The AIFMD provides an EU-wide harmonised framework for monitoring and supervising risks posed by AIFMs and the AIFs they manage. In addition, it aims to strengthen the internal AIF market.

The AIFMD provides rules on the

(i)   regulatory capital which is required when licensed as an AIFM

(ii)   delegation of tasks to third parties

(iii)   valuation of AIFs

(iv)   organisational structure of the AIFM

(v)   authorisation of the AIFM

(vi)   passporting of AIFs in the EU

(vii) appointment of the depositary

(viii) risk management

(ix)   acquisition of control over non-listed companies and

(x)   reporting to investors and to Competent Authorities

The AIFMD draft was approved by the European Parliament on 11 November 2010 and the text of the directive was published in the Official Journal of the European Parliament on 1 July 2011.

The directive came into force on 21 July 2011 starting a two-year implementation time frame. All Member States of the European Union were required to transpose the directive into national law by 22 July 2013.

1.3)   The position of Directives in EU Law:

EU directives lay down certain end results that must be achieved in every Member State. National authorities have to adapt their laws to meet these goals, but they are free to decide how to do so. Directives are used to bring different national laws in line and are particularly common in matters affecting the operation of the single market. The European Union is based on the rule of law. This means that every action taken by the EU is founded on treaties that have been approved voluntarily and democratically by all EU member countries. The Treaty of Lisbon increased the number of policy areas where 'Ordinary Legislative Procedure' is used. The European Parliament also has more power to block a proposal if it

disagrees with the Council. The EU's standard decision-making procedure is known as 'Ordinary Legislative Procedure'. This means that the directly elected European Parliament has to approve EU legislation together with the Council (the governments of the 28 EU countries). The Commission drafts and implements EU legislation. EU-Law – which has equal force with national law – confers rights and obligations on the authorities in each Member State, as well as on individuals and businesses. The authorities in each Member State are responsible for implementing EU legislation into national law and enforcing it correctly, and they must guarantee citizens' rights under these laws.

1.4)   The AIFMD Implementation Regulation:

Like most of the directives issued by the European Union, the AIFMD Directive is supplemented by an Implementation Directive (Commission Delegated Regulation 231/2013 EC) issued by the European Commission. The right to issue additional legislation is directly derived from the AIFMD Directive itself, which enforces the European Commission to issues rules relating to:

(i)   calculation of the threshold;

(ii)   leverage;

(iii)   operating conditions for Alternative Investment Fund Managers;

(iv)   risk and liquidity management;

(v)   valuation;

(vi)   delegation;

(vii)   requirements detailing the functions and duties of depositaries of Alternative Investment Funds

(viii) rules on transparency;

(ix)   specific requirements relating to third countries. It is important to note that all these supplementing rules begin to apply at the same time as Directive 2011/61/EU.

1.5)   The position of Regulations in EU law:

Regulations are the most direct form of EU law – as soon as they are passed, they have binding legal force throughout every Member State, on a par with national laws. National governments do not have to take action themselves to implement EU regulations. They are different from directives, which are addressed to national authorities, who must then take action to make them part of national law, and decisions, which apply in specific cases only, involving particular authorities or individuals. Regulations are passed either jointly by the EU Council and European Parliament, or by the Commission alone.

1.6)   Other documents building the AIFMD framework:

In the meantime, the European legislators have passed a couple of additional Regulations, such as

(i)   Implementing Regulation No. 447/2013, covering the criteria and obligations for opting in under AIFMD (2 pages);

(ii)   Commission Implementing Regulation No. 448/2013, detailing requirements with regards to the Member State of Reference assessment (3 pages);

(iii)   Commission Delegated Regulation supplementing Directive 2011/61/EU, detailing the different types of Alternative Investment Funds;

(iv)   ESMA Guidelines on key concepts of the AIFMD (7 pages); and ESMA Questions and Answers Application of the AIFMD (7 pages).

Together with AIFM Directive 2011/61/EU (73 pages) and the Implementation Regulation 231/2013/EU (95 pages), the AIFMD framework is made up of 187 pages of documentation with a regulatory impact.

1.7)   National interpretation:

Due to the fact that many topics addressed in the AIFM Directive are also covered by Implementation or Delegated Regulations, the room for national legislators to introduce specific rules is limited, and according to AIFM Directive 2011/61/EU stricter rules can expressly only be introduced in specific areas. This means that, with some exceptions, the AIFMD framework implementation should be similar in most Member States.

1.8)   Consequences of not implementing the rules:

If upon expiry of the deadline for implementation, the Directive has not yet been correctly and fully implemented, several consequences can arise.

(i)   Even if not yet fully/correctly implemented, those provisions in the Directive that are directly applicable (i.e. their content is unconditional and sufficiently precise) may be invoked by undertakings or citizens against the defaulting Member State and must be applied by national courts and administrations as it regards the relationships between individuals and the State.

(ii)   National law must be interpreted in conformity with the Directive. In this context, and if needed, national judges may, or, if giving a final decision, must refer a preliminary question to the Court of Justice of the European Union, asking for guidance about the interpretation of the relevant provisions of the Directive.

(iii) Individuals may file court actions to recover the damages caused by a sufficiently serious breach (including non-implementation) of a Directive by Member States (at the national, regional or local level). A breach of a provision is deemed sufficiently serious when the transposition is completely lacking or when the directive provision that has been belatedly or incorrectly implemented leaves Member States considerably reduced or no discretion in implementing that provision.

(iv)   A judgment by the Court of Justice of the European Union finding that a Member State has violated a Community Directive is not only significant in that it ascertains a violation of the law and the Member State concerned must comply with it. If the violation persists, it is also the prerequisite for action by the Commission aiming at condemnation by the ECJ of the defaulting Member State to the payment of penalties and/or lump sums – since the entry into force of the Lisbon Treaty, the Commission may ask for penalties and/or lump sums directly in infringement proceedings if the Member State fails to comply with its obligation to take measures to transpose a directive adopted under a legislative procedure such as the Services Directive. Such a judgment also allows individuals to easily prove the sufficiently serious character of an infringement of Community law in actions for State liability.

1.9) Funds potentially captured by the AIF definition:[1]

Country	Estimates of entities captured by the definition of AIF in Article 4(1)(a) of the AIFMD
Austria	About 970 funds
Belgium	About 120 funds
Czech Republic	About 160 funds
Finland	250-300 funds
France	9,000-12,000 funds
Germany	About 4,000 funds
Greece	—
Hungary	About 520 funds
Iceland	50-60 funds
Ireland	More than 2,100 funds
Italy	About 660 funds
Latvia	20-25 funds
Liechtenstein	About 400 funds
Lithuania	Up to 20 funds
Luxembourg	At least 2,000 funds
Malta	Less than 500 funds
Netherlands	About 1,400 funds
Norway	At least 170 funds
Portugal	About 450 funds
Slovak Republic	20-30 funds
Slovenia	About 10 funds
Spain	About 330 funds
Sweden	500-750 funds
UK	Approximately 2,000 funds
Between approximately 25,650 and 28,975 funds	

---

[1] ESMA, Final report, Guidelines on key concepts of the AIFMD, page 24

2.0) Capital requirements:

Directive	Title	Article/Paragraph
2011/61/EU	Directive on Alternative Investment Fund Managers	§ 23 (introduction) Article 4, §2 Article 9
231/2013	COMMISSION DELEGATED REGULATION on exemptions, general operating conditions, depositaries, leverage, transparency and supervision	Article 14 Article 15
2009/65/EC	Directive on the coordination of laws, regulations and administrative provisions relating to undertakings for collective investment in transferable securities (UCITS)	Article 7
2006/48/EC	Directive relating to the taking up and pursuit of the business of credit institutions	Article 56 -67
2006/49/EC	Directive on the capital adequacy of investment firms and credit institutions	Article 21

Key requirements:

- Externally managed AIFMs and Super ManCos must provide 125,000 EUR of initial own funds
- Internally managed AIFMs must provide 300,000 EUR of initial own funds
- For AuMs exceeding 250 million EUR, AIFMs must provide 0.02% of additional own funds
- For professional liability risk AIFMs must provide 0.01% in capital for all AuMs
- Based on the loss history, Competent Authorities can increase or decrease the capital requirement

2.1) Capital types to be provided:

Under the AIFMD there are three different types of capital requirements:

(i) Initial own funds of 125,000 EUR must be provided regardless of the AuMs an AIFM manages.

(ii) In case the AuMs exceed the amount of 250 million EUR the AIFM has to provide additional own funds of 0.02% on the amounts exceeding 250 million EUR. This means that every million of additional AuMs requires a capital increase of 200 EUR up to a point where the total capital of the AIFM reaches the amount of 10 million EUR. Up to 50% of additional own funds can be provided in form of guarantees issued by a Credit Institution or Insurance Company with a registered office in the EU or in a third country where the regulatory rules are deemed to be equal to EU law.

(iii)   Additional own funds of 0.01% of the AuMs must be provide to cover professional liability risk. It is important to note that this additional 100 EUR per million of AuM must be provided for all AuMs and neither the threshold of 250 million EUR nor the threshold of 10 million EUR is applicable. The Competent Authorities of the AIFM's Home Member State can lower or increase the capital requirement to cover professional liability risk if the loss history of the last three years provides adequate justification. The amount to be provided should never fall below 0.008%, which is equal to 8 EUR per million of AuMs. The value of the portfolios of AIFs managed is the sum of the absolute value of all assets of all AIFs managed by the AIFM, including assets acquired through use of leverage, whereby derivative instruments must be valued at their market value.

Article 21 of Directive 2006/49/EC (the capital adequacy of investment firms and credit institutions) adds another check to ensure that a minimum capital level is available at all times. The AIFM must check on a regular basis whether the own funds are lower than 25% of the preceding year's fixed overhead. If this should be the case the capital buffer has to be filled accordingly.

2.2) Initial own funds and internally managed AIFs:

An internally managed AIF is a self-managed structure where the fund is both an AIF and an AIFM. AIFs should be deemed internally managed when the management functions are performed by the governing body or any other internal resource of the AIF. Where the legal form of the AIF permits internal management and where the AIF's governing body chooses not to appoint an external AIFM, the AIF is also an AIFM. With regard to initial own funds, the European legislation clearly differentiates between AIFMs which are internally and externally managed. Internally managed AIFs must provide initial own funds of 300,000 EUR compared to the 125,000 EUR externally managed AIFs must provide, an increase of 140%.

2.3) Exception for Super-ManCos:

A Super-ManCo is an AIFM that owns a license under the AIFMD and under UCITS and consequently can manage retail funds as well as alternative funds. In this case the AIFMD applies the capital calculation rules of the UCITS Directive 2009/65/EU, where capital requirements are defined under Article 7. UCITS makes no distinction between internally and externally managed AIFs, which leads to the consequence that Super-ManCos just need to provide 125,000 EUR of initial own funds plus 0.02% of additional own funds for AuM amounts exceeding the threshold of 250 million EUR. The AIFMD requirements with regard to additional own funds for covering professional liability risk still apply to Super-ManCos.

2.4) Insurance coverage instead of additional own funds for liability risk:

Instead of providing the additional own funds to cover professional liability risk, the AIFM can chose to provide insurance coverage. To do so a couple of conditions must be met:

(i) the initial duration of the contract must be at least one year;

(ii) the notice period for dismissing the contract should be at least 90 days;

(iii) the coverage must be provided by an entity which is licensed to do so under EU law;

(iv) the provider must be a third-party entity;

(v) any agreed defined excess shall be fully covered by own funds.

The insurance coverage for an individual claim shall be equal to at least 0.7% and the coverage of the insurance for claims in aggregate per year shall be equal to at least 0.9% of the value of the portfolios of AIFs managed by the AIFM.[2] The adequacy of the insurance contract must be reviewed at least annually.

2.5) Definition and management of own funds:

With regard to the definition of own funds, the AIFMD references Articles 56–67 of the EU Credit Institutions Directive 2006/48/EC. According to article 57:

(i)   paid up capital, plus share premium accounts but excluding cumulative preferential shares;

(ii)   reserves and profits and losses brought forward;

(iii)   funds for general banking risks;

(iv)   revaluation reserves;

(v)   value adjustments;

(vi)   fixed-term cumulative preferential shares;

(vii)   subordinated loan capital

can be used to fulfil capital requirements. Items like;

(i)   own shares at book value;

(ii)   intangible assets;

(iii)   material losses of the current financial year;

(iv)   subordinated claims

are deemed not suitable and need to be excluded from the calculation. Own funds, including any additional own funds, shall be invested in liquid assets or assets readily convertible to cash in the short term and shall not include speculative positions.

3.0) Delegation:

Directive	Title	Article/Paragraph
2011/61/EU	Directive on Alternative Investment Fund Managers	§9 (introduction) Article 19 Article 20
231/2013	COMMISSION DELE-GATED REGULATION on exemptions, general operating conditions, de-positaries, leverage, trans-parency and supervision	Article 75 Article 76 Article 77 Article 78 Article 79 Article 80 Article 81 Article 82

<u>Key requirements:</u>

– In general, delegation and sub-delegation is allowed under the AIFMD

– There must be objective reasons for the delegation and it should not circumvent AIFMD rules

– The delegate must be of good repute and should have the required skills and resources

– The AIFM must perform due diligence on the vendor, including a conflicts of interest assessment

– The AIFM must have the right to direct and inspect the delegate at any time

3.1) Introduction to delegation:

The general concept of delegation under the AIFMD is addressed in Section 8 of Directive 2011/61/EC. Subject to specific limitations and obligations, an AIFM is generally allowed to delegate some of its functions to third parties, which may be based outside of the EU. Before the delegation arrangement becomes effective the AIFM has to notify the Competent Authorities. The limitations and obligations depend on the type of function outsourced. Specific requirements apply with regard to the delegation of risk and portfolio management. Delegation rules can be clustered into five sub-categories:

(i) general principles;

(ii) the contract with the delegate;

(iii) the due diligence on the delegate;

(iv)   the conflicts of interest assessment with regard to dele-
        gation;

(v)   sub-delegation.

3.2)   General delegation requirements:

3.2.1)   Letter box entity:

One of the specific concerns of the AIFMD is to prevent the use
of 'letterbox' entities. The regulation specifies that measures
would be adopted when an entity is deemed to constitute a letterbox entity. Consequently it would no longer be considered to be
an AIF. Accordingly, there are a couple of relevant circumstances
to be taken into consideration. Key considerations in this regard
include that:

(i)   the AIFM no longer retains the necessary expertise and
        resources to supervise the delegated tasks effectively
        and manage the risks associated with the delegation;

(ii)   the AIFM loses its contractual rights to inquire, in-
        spect, have access or give instructions to its delegates
        or the exercise of such rights becomes impossible in
        practice;

(iii)   the AIFM delegates the performance of investment
        management functions to an extent that exceeds by a
        substantial margin the investment management func-
        tions performed by the AIFM itself.

Under the AIFMD the investment management function consists of risk and portfolio management. The AIFM should at least retain one of these functions to ensure compliance with this requirement.

3.2.2) Objective reasons for delegation:

The AIFM must provide the Competent Authorities with a detailed description, explanation and evidence of objective reasons for the delegation. An objective reason might be:

(i)   the optimisation of business functions and processes;

(ii)   cost saving;

(iii)   the expertise of the delegate in administration or in specific markets or investments;

(iv)   access of the delegate to global trading capabilities.

3.2.3) Ultimate responsibility of the AIFM:

One of the main concepts the AIFMD establishes is that of the ultimate responsibility and liability of the AIFM. It does not matter how many tasks were outsourced to third-party vendors. The front to back responsibility towards the AIFs, the investors and the regulators always stays with the AIFM. Therefore the overall delegation structure should never circumvent the AIFM's responsibility or liability. Such circumvention might occur where the contractual situation between the AIF and the AIFM on the one hand, and between the AIFM and the delegate on the other hand, refers the AIF and its investors directly to the delegate with regard to compensation requests for any wrongdoing. An even more generic requirement establishes the rule that the delegation should not undermine the AIFMD conditions for authorisation. The main condition is to be compliant with all rules defined under the AIFM Directive and related regulations, which does not really help to interpret this rule. To enhance our understanding with regard to the meaning, we need to remember why AIFMD was established. At the G20 Summit in November 2008, world leaders agreed that as a consequence of the financial market crises all significant markets and market participants should act under adequate regulation and supervision. To improve market stability, transparency and integrity it was decided to enhance regulatory regimes, prudential oversight and risk management.[3] Consequently, undermining the conditions for authorisation would

mean choosing a delegation set-up which circumvents the effective oversight and the application of regulation. This could be the case whenever delegation is systematically used to deny regulators access to information and documents necessary to carry out their oversight function.

---

[3] DECLARATION, SUMMIT ON FINANCIAL MARKETS AND THE WORLD ECONOMY, November 15, 2008

3.3)   Contract with the delegate:

The AIFM must ensure continuity of the delegated tasks. In case the delegate terminates the contract or goes out of business the AIFM must be in a position to conduct its business without any interruption.

The contract between the AIFM and the delegate must be in writing and should enable the AIFM to instruct and inspect the delegate at any time. Mandatory content building blocks are listed under Commission Delegated Regulation 231/2013, Art. 75d, which defines that provisions with regard to:

(i)   business continuity management (BCM),

(ii)   data protection,

(iii)   sub-delegation, and

(iv)   the conditions for termination and the duration of the contract

must be an integral part of every contract between the AIFM and the delegate. The AIFM must ensure on an initial and ongoing basis that delegates operate within the boundaries of the applicable law and it must carry out an effective supervision at all times.

3.4)   Vendor due diligence:

3.4.1)   Vendor skills and reputation check:

Before any kind of delegation can take place the AIFM must execute a series of checks with regard to the delegate, who must have
sufficient resources to conduct the delegated tasks. The delegate's
staff must be of good reputation and should possess the required
skills. The reputation assessment should include checks on:

(i)   criminal records,

(ii)   bankruptcy,

(iii)   insolvency,

(iv)   judicial proceedings,

(v)   administrative sanctions,

(vi)   money laundering and

(vii)   criminal investigations.

In case tasks are outsourced to large companies with several hun-
dred employees, it might be not possible for the AIFM to check
them all. Consequently, it might be sufficient to execute the
named background checks on leading employees. Additionally,
the AIFM should review the employee on-boarding process of the
delegates.

3.4.2)   Potential prevention of effective supervision:

Somehow the EU legislators anticipated that task outsourcing
might be used to circumvent specific AIFMD rules and the effective supervision by Competent Authorities. Article 79 of Com-

mission Delegated Regulation 231/2013 introduces an assessment methodology which provides objective criteria to determine whether a specific delegation is deemed to be not compliant with AIFMD. If:

(i)   the AIFM, its auditors and the Competent Authorities do not have effective access to data related to the delegated functions and to the business premises of the delegate;

(ii)   the Competent Authorities are not able to exercise those rights of access;

(iii)   the delegate does not cooperate with the Competent Authorities;

(iv)   and the AIFM does not make available to the Competent Authorities upon request all information necessary to enable them to supervise, the delegation is considered not to be in line with AIFMD.

3.4.3) Delegation of risk and portfolio management:

If the AIFM wants to confer risk or portfolio management to a third party it must ensure that the delegate is adequately licensed in the European Union. Risk and portfolio management can be outsourced to:

(i)   management companies authorised under Directive 2009/65/EC;[4]

---

[4] UCITS Directive

(ii)   investment   firms   authorised   under   Directive
        2004/39/EC[5] to perform portfolio management;

(iii)   credit   institutions   authorised   under   Directive
        2006/48/EC[6] having the authorisation to perform port-
        folio management under Directive 2004/39/EC;

(iv)   external   AIFMs   authorised   under   Directive
        2011/61/EU;[7]

(v)   third-country entities authorised or registered for the
        purpose of asset management and effectively super-
        vised by a Competent Authority in those countries.

If the delegate is a third-country entity additional conditions must
be fulfilled. A written arrangement between the AIFM's Competent Authorities and the supervisory authorities of the delegate is
required and should allow Competent Authorities to:

(i)   obtain upon request relevant information and docu-
        ments necessary to carry out the supervisory tasks;

(ii)   carry out on-site inspections on the premises of the
        delegate;

(iii)   receive information from the supervisory authority in
        the third country to investigate AIFMD breaches;

(iv)   cooperate in enforcement in case of AIFMD breaches.

---

[5] MIFID I

[6] Taking up and pursuit of the business of credit institutions

[7] AIFMD

3.4.4)   Conflicts of interest assessment:

For each delegation a two-step conflicts of interest assessment must be conducted. The AIFM has to clarify whether there are any potential conflicts and whether they are correctly disclosed.

If the AIFM or the AIF and the delegate are members of the same group it must be assessed to which extent the delegate controls the AIFM or the AIF. The AIFM must also assess the likelihood that the delegate:

(i)   makes a financial gain, or avoids a financial loss, at the expense of the AIF or the investor;

(ii)   has an interest in the outcome of a service or an activity provided to the AIFM or the AIF;

(iii)   has an incentive to favour the interest of a client over the interests of the AIF;

(iv)   will receive from a third party an inducement in relation to the collective PM activities.

If any of these applies, the AIFM must ensure proper disclosure. He also has to ensure that the delegate takes all reasonable steps to identify, manage and monitor potential conflicts of interest. The delegate should have procedures and policies in place to discover, disclose, manage and monitor conflicts of interest, and if prevention is not possible he must also ensure proper disclosure.

The portfolio and the risk management function must always be functionally and hierarchically separated. If they are delegated to a third party, the delegate has to prove that it follows AIFMD separation requirements. Risk and portfolio management functions are deemed to be properly separated if:

(i)   persons engaged in PM tasks are not engaged in the performance of conflicting tasks such as controlling;

(ii)   persons engaged in risk management tasks are not engaged in conflicting operating tasks and are not supervised by staff responsible for operating tasks;

(iii) the separation is ensured throughout the whole hierarchical structure of the delegate up to its governing body.

3.5) Sub-delegation:

Generally the delegate is allowed to further delegate tasks. An exception is the appointed external valuer. The external valuer should not delegate the valuation function to a third party. Prior to the sub–delegation, the AIFM must consent in writing. A general consent in advance is not acceptable. The AIFM must notify Competent Authorities about the sub-delegation and must adhere to minimum content requirements. The delegate must execute all checks on the sub-delegate which are usually executed by the AIFM in relation to its delegates.

4.0) Valuations:

Directive	Title	Article / Paragraph
2011/61/EU	Directive on Alternative Investment Fund Managers	Article 19
231/2013	COMMISSION DELEGATED REGULATION on exemptions, general operating conditions, depositaries, leverage, transparency and supervision	Article 67 Article 68 Article 69 Article 70 Article 71 Article 72

Key requirements:

– The AIFM can either carry out the valuer function itself, or it can delegate it to a third party
– If the valuer function is delegated to a third party all delegation requirements apply
– The job of the valuer can but does not need to include the NAV calculation
– The valuation minimum interval is annually but must be in line with subscription and redemption policy
– The AIFM must have valuation policies and procedures in place for all assets it is dealing with

4.1)   Who can act as a valuer:

In general the AIFM has the choice to either carry out the valuation function itself or to appoint an external valuer. If it decides to conduct the valuation function internally, it is required to establish a complete functional and hierarchical separation from all other business functions like portfolio and risk management. Whenever the AIFM appoints an external valuer, the AIFMD stipulates that sub-delegation of the valuation function to a third party is not allowed. Competent authorities might request that the AIFM demonstrate that the external valuer is professionally recognised and can provide professional guarantees. The term professional guarantees, which is defined under Commission Delegated Regulation 231/2013, means that the external valuer should be able to demonstrate, by providing written evidence, that it is capable and qualified enough to properly carry out the role of independent external valuer. With regard to the valuer selection process, the AIFM has to follow delegation rules. Under AIFMD there is a clear distinction between calculating the NAV of an AIF and the role of the valuer. Whenever the NAV calculation is delegated to an external administrator, he is not considered to be a valuer, which allows the AIFM to either retain this function or to delegate it to another third party.

4.2)   Minimum frequency requirements:

For all kinds of alternative investment funds, the NAV calculation must take place at least once a year. For open-ended AIFs the
NAV calculation frequency needs to be in line with the
redemption policy, and for closed-ended funds the NAV calculation must be triggered in line with capital increases or decreases.
The European legislation requires that whenever the NAV is calculated, the number of units and shares also needs to be con-
firmed and the NAV must be communicated to investors.

4.3)   Valuation policies and procedures:

The AIFM must ensure that valuation policies and procedures are
maintained for each AIF for which it has management responsibility. They must be available in writing and should follow minimum form and content requirements. Valuation policies and procedures must be applied in a consistent manner and they should
be reviewed at least annually. The policy should identify and implement the methodology used for each asset type and should
define roles and responsibilities, such as:

(i)   competence of personnel,

(ii)   controls to be executed,

(iii)   escalation channels,

(iv)   and rules for valuation adjustments

In addition, it must describe the methodology and the selection
criteria used for the assessment of available valuation models and
sources. Valuation models always must be verified by a person

with sufficient expertise and need to be signed off by the AIFM's senior management. Communication channels between the AIFM and the appointed external valuer must be agreed and a review process must be implemented for assets where a material risk of inappropriate valuation exists. Another important mandatory

part of the valuation policies are the procedures for remediating wrong valuations and NAV calculations, which means that there must be a detailed process for how to change the figures. Changes made to valuation policies and procedures must be reviewed and signed off by the risk function and the senior management of the AIFM.

4.4)   Other valuation-related requirements:

Generally the AIF is not allowed to invest in a specific type of assets unless the valuation methodology has been identified and the valuation policies and procedures have been adjusted accordingly. Sources for further rules with regard to valuation could be the national law of the AIFM's Home Member State and the AIF rules as defined in the prospectus or its instruments of incorporation. In line with delegation requirements, the AIFM must execute an initial and periodic due diligence on the external valuer. Under the AIFMD it is always the AIFM who is responsible and liable towards the AIF and its investors with regard to the proper valuation, the correct NAV calculation and the timely NAV publication. The appointment of an external valuer cannot change this fact, but nevertheless the appointed external valuer is liable towards the AIFM for any losses suffered as a result of the external valuer's negligence or intentional failure. This liability is irrespective of any contractual arrangements.

5.0) Organisational requirements:

Directive	Title	Article/Paragraph
2011/61/EU	Directive on Alternative Investment Fund Managers	§22 (introduction)
		§24 (introduction)
		§29 (introduction)
		§32 (Introduction)
		Article 12
		Article 13
		Article 14
		Article 15
		Article 19
		Article 29
231/2013	COMMISSION DELE-GATED REGULATION on exemptions, general operating conditions, depositaries, leverage, transparency and supervision	Article 17
		Article 23 - 28
		Article 30
		Article 31
		Article 33
		Article 34
		Article 35
		Article 36
		Article 37
		Article 57
		Article 58
		Article 59
		Article 60 - 66
		Article 80

- The AIFM must have a policy on how to identify, manage and disclose conflicts of interest
- It is required to set up the following functions: (i) risk management, (ii) compliance and (iii) audit
- Some functions must be functionally and hierarchically separated from daily operations
- Data security and BCM measures must be implemented to avoid operational break downs
- Various remuneration requirements must be regarded (AIFMD, ESMA, Regulation 2009/384/EC)

5.1) Conflicts of interest:

5.1.1) Organisational precautions:

The AIFMD requires AIFMs to be organized in a way which minimizes conflicts of interests. For example, this might require the setting up of information barriers and effective procedures to prevent or control the exchange of information between relevant persons engaged in collective portfolio management. The same applies for all other business areas where the exchange of information may harm the interest of one or more AIFs or their investors. The separation of supervision lines is listed under the AIFMD as an instrument to avoid organizational conflicts of interests. Remuneration links, meaning links between the performance and the compensation of business units where the link

in remuneration might create conflicts of interest, should be re-
moved.

5.1.2)   Conflicts of interest policy:

Beside the basic organizational side of things, the EU legislation
also requires the establishment of a number of other mechanisms
which can help to avoid disadvantages for AIFs and their investors. First of all, AIFMs must introduce a written conflicts of interest policy defining detailed procedures with regard to the identification, the management and the disclosure of conflicts of interest. Article 30 of Delegated Regulation 231/2013 offers specific guidance for the identification process.

5.1.3)   Identification of conflicts of interests:

The AIFMD stipulates that the AIFM especially has to take into
account cases where a relevant person or a person directly or indirectly linked by way of control to the AIFM:

(i)   is likely to make a financial gain, or avoid a financial
         loss, at the expense of the AIF or its investors;

(ii)   has an interest in the outcome of a service or an activi-
         ty provided to the AIF or its investors or to a client or a
         transaction carried out on behalf of the AIF or a client,
         which is distinct from the AIF's interest in that out-
         come;

(iii)   has a financial or other incentive to favour the interest
         of a UCITS, a client or group of clients or another AIF
         over the interest of the AIF or the interests of one

investor over the interests of another investor or group of investors in the same AIF;

(iv) carries out the same activities for the AIF and for another AIF, a UCITS or a client;

(v) receives or will receive from a person other than the AIF or its investors an inducement in relation to collective portfolio management activities provided to the AIF, in the form of monies, goods or services other than the standard commission or fee for that service.

5.1.4) Conflicts of interest disclosures:

Whenever conflicts of interest cannot be avoided they must be disclosed to investors. To this end the AIFM must maintain and regularly update a record of conflicts of interest entailing all material risks for the investor. The structure of the record must follow the definition of the different types of conflicts of interest as detailed under Article 32 of Commission Delegated Regulation 231/2013 and AIFMD Article 14, § 1 a-e. The two provisions structure conflicts of interest as follows:

(i) conflicts with regard to open-ended funds between investors leaving the fund and investors which stay invested;

(ii) conflicts between the AIFM, including its managers and employees, and the AIF or its investors;

(iii) conflicts between two different AIFs or their investors;

(iv)   conflicts between the AIF and a UCITS managed by the AIFM or its investors;

(v)   conflicts between two clients of the AIFM.

The senior management of the AIFM must receive on an ongoing basis and at least annually a report on all activities containing conflicts of interest. Where conflicts of interest cannot be avoided with a relatively high level of confidence they must be disclosed to investors before they invest. A durable medium must be used for the disclosure. Experience shows that there are different interpretations in national AIFMD laws for the definition of the term 'durable medium'. While in Luxembourg it is enough to disclose conflicts of interests on a web page, which means theoretically a USB stick or a hard disk might satisfy the requirement of a durable medium, German regulators also require publishing on paper, which means that the disclosure will most likely be part of the prospectus or the annual report. If a website is used the investor must be notified about its existence, the information must always be up to date and the site must be continuously accessible.

5.2)   Rules on establishing AIFM functions:

5.2.1) Separation requirements:

Separation requirements exist with regard to:

(i)   the safekeeping function,

(ii)   the valuation function,

(iii)   and the risk management function

For each AIF managed by an AIFM, a single depositary other than the AIFM must be appointed. Investors' assets must be clearly separated from the AIFM's assets. If an external valuer has not been appointed, the valuation of assets and the NAV calculation should be functionally and hierarchically independent from the portfolio management function. Also, the risk management function must be functionally and hierarchically separated from all other operating units. Commission Delegated Regulation 231/2013 under Article 80 / §2 offers an assessment methodology which allows to test whether the separation was established in line with AIFMD requirements. The portfolio or risk management function may be considered to be functionally and hierarchically separated from other potentially conflicting tasks if:

(i) persons engaged in portfolio management tasks are not engaged in the performance of potentially conflicting tasks such as controlling tasks;

(ii) persons engaged in risk management tasks are not engaged in the performance of potentially conflicting tasks such as operating tasks;

(iii) persons engaged in risk management functions are not supervised by those responsible for the performance of operating tasks.

5.2.2) Set-up of independent control functions:

The AIFMD requires each AIFM to set up 4 different independent control functions, namely:

(i) a Senior Management or Supervisory Function,

(ii)   a Compliance Function,

(iii)   an Audit Function,

(iv)   and a Risk Management Function (the Risk Management Function will be discussed in a later chapter)

The role of the Supervisory Function is to implement the general investment policy and the valuation policy and to ensure an effective compliance function. In addition, it must execute a couple of periodic checks and reviews, in particular with regard to the general investment policy, the investment strategy, the risk limits, internal procedures for investment decision making and the risk management policy including risk limits. Another important task is the definition and the implementation of an adequate remuneration policy. The Supervisory Function must receive frequently written reports on compliance, internal audit, risk management and investment strategy implementation. The independent Compliance Function must monitor the adequacy and effectiveness of the AIFM's policies and procedures and should advise persons responsible for carrying out services and activities with regard to compliance with the AIFMD. It must have the necessary authority, resources and expertise to effectively carry out its tasks. The Compliance Function must report frequently, but at least annually, to the senior management on compliance matters. Persons in the Compliance Function are not allowed to be involved in any kind of operating tasks, like the production of services to clients, as this would limit its effectiveness and might create conflicts of interest. The way the remuneration of the compliance function is defined should not impact or limit its objectivity. With regard to the Audit Function, the AIFMD only applies a very limited set of requirements. An audit plan must be maintained and recommendations must be issued. The Audit Function must verify the compliance with its recommendations and should report audit matters to senior management.

5.3) Minimum company infrastructure and transaction processing requirements:

5.3.1) Data security, business continuity and documentation of company structure:

Data security is critical for most AIFM businesses, as nowadays data processing is fully electronic. Information assets such as client information, payment information, personal files, bank account details etc. might be hard to replace once lost and might be a potential threat if they fall into the wrong hands. The AIFMD requires implementing processes, measures and precautions to minimise the associated risk for AIFs and their investors. Consequently, AIFMs must implement systems and procedures which ensure data security. BCM plans must also be in place to ensure the timely resumption of services and activities without material loss of data. The AIFM must maintain records of all portfolio transactions and specific attributes must be recorded depending on the type of transaction. In addition, records must be maintained for subscriptions and redemptions. Portfolio transactions, subscription and redemption records must be stored for at least

5 years if there are no stricter record retention requirements under national law. The storage medium must allow access to the information in the future and a full audit trail must be ensured.

AIFMs must document and implement:

(i)   an organisational structure,

(ii)   roles & responsibilities,

(iii)   the decision-making processes,

(iv)   internal control mechanisms,

(v)   communication flows,

(vi)   and reporting flows

Records must be maintained for all documents mentioned above. Accounting policies and procedures that allow identifying all assets and liabilities of an AIF must be in place.

5.3.2) Using prime brokers, order aggregation, corporate actions:

When using prime brokers there must be a written contract defining the details and conditions for the reuse of assets like securities lending. The depositary must be informed about the prime broker contract and due diligence must be conducted in accordance with delegation provisions.

Aggregating AIF orders with orders from other AIFs, UCITS or own orders is allowed if:

(i)   the aggregation of orders will not work overall to the disadvantage of any AIF, UCITS or clients whose order is to be aggregated;

(ii)   an order allocation policy is established and implemented, providing in sufficiently precise terms for the fair allocation of aggregated orders, including how the volume and price of orders determines allocations and the treatment of partial executions.

The aggregation should not work to the disadvantage of any AIF or UCITS. In the case of aggregation and partial execution of the orders of clients, UCITS or AIFs must always have priority.

AIFMs must develop a strategy for executing voting rights held in the AIFs. The strategy must define:

(i)   the monitoring of corporate actions,

(ii)   how to ensure that the execution is in line with the investment objectives,

(iii)   and how to prevent conflicts of interests

A summary description of the strategy must be made available to investors at their request. With regard to subscriptions and redemptions, the AIFMD defines a set of minimum requirements. The investor must be informed about every subscription and redemption by means of a durable medium. As we already learned from previous chapters, the definition of a durable medium can differ from Member State to Member State. The information provided on such transactions must contain specific minimum attributes, namely:

(i)   the identification of the AIFM,

(ii)   the identification of the investor,

(iii)   the date and time of receipt of the order,

(iv)   the date of execution,

(v)   the identification of the AIF,

(vi)   the gross value of the order including charges for sub-
       scription or the net amount after charges for redemp-
       tions

At the request of the investor, the AIFM must provide order sta-
tus information.

5.4)   Remuneration:

5.4.1) Remuneration requirements of Annex II, AIFMD:

The AIFMD's Annex II offers concrete guidance with regard to
the definition of the remuneration policy and introduces a set of
basic concepts which must be an integral part of this policy. The
most important concept for AIFMs might be the proportionality
approach, which allows them to comply with the rules in a way
and to the extent that is appropriate to their size, internal organi-
zation and the nature, scope and complexity of their activities.
Annex II does not define the criteria to be used for defining exactly what kind of AIFM can dis-apply which rules. This was done
by ESMA when issuing its guidance on remuneration for AIFMs
(please see section 5.4.3). Specific requirements with regard to
the remuneration policy are listed in the table below.

Topic	Policy Requirements
Effective risk management	-Should not encourage risk-taking which is inconsistent with the risk pro files of the AIFs
Conflicts of interest	-Must be in line with the business strategy of the AIFM and AIFs -Must include measures to avoid conflicts of interest
Periodical management reviews	-The management body periodically reviews the general principles
Annual central and independent internal review for compliance	-Implementation must be subject to central and independent internal review at least annually for compliance with policies and procedures
Control functions compensation	-Control functions compensation must be in line with their objectives -Control functions compensation must be independent of the performance of the business areas they control
Remuneration of the senior officers in the risk management and com-	-Remuneration of the senior officers in the risk management and compliance functions must be directly overseen by the remuneration committee

Topic	Policy Requirements
pliance functions	
Performance-related remuneration	The total amount of remuneration should be based on a combination of: -The individual performance (financial and non-financial performance) -The performance the business unit or AIF concerned -The overall results of the AIFM, and when assessing individual performance
Multi-year frame-work	-Performance should be set in a multi-year framework -Assessment process must be based on longer-term performance -Actual payment of performance-based components must be spread over a period which takes into account the redemption policy of the AIFs it manages and their investment risks
Guaranteed variable remuneration	-Guaranteed variable remuneration should be exceptional, occur only in the context of hiring new staff and limited to the first year
Fixed and variable	-Appropriate balance between the

Topic	Policy Requirements
components of total remuneration	variable and the fixed component -Fixed part must represent a sufficiently high proportion -Fully flexible policy on variable remuneration components, including the possibility to pay no variable remuneration component
Early termination	-Payments related to the early termination of a contract reflect performance achieved over time and are designed in a way that does not reward failure
Adjustment mechanism	-The measurement of performance used to calculate variable remuneration components or pools of variable remuneration components includes a comprehensive adjustment mechanism to integrate all relevant types of current and future risks
Variable remuneration and shares of the AIF	-A substantial portion, but at least 50%, Of any variable remuneration, consists of units or shares of the AIF concerned, or equivalent ownership interests, or

Topic	Policy Requirements
	share-linked instruments or equivalent non-cash instruments -An exception is if the management of AIFs accounts for less than 50% of the total portfolio managed by the AIFM
Appropriate retention policy	-The pay in shares should be subject to an appropriate retention policy -Competent Authorities may place restrictions on the types and designs of those instruments or ban certain instruments as appropriate
Deferral period	-A substantial portion, but at least 40%, of the variable remuneration component is deferred over a period which is appropriate in view of the life cycle and redemption policy of the AIF concerned -The period shall be at least three to 5 years unless the life cycle of the AIF concerned is shorter -Remuneration payable under deferral arrangements vests no faster than on

Topic	Policy Requirements
	a pro-rata basis -In the case of a variable remuneration component of a particularly high amount, at least 60% of the amount is deferred
Payment or vesting of variable remuneration	-The variable remuneration, including the deferred portion, is paid or vests only if it is sustainable according to the financial situation of the AIFM and justified by the performance of the business unit, the AIF and the individual concerned -The total variable remuneration shall generally be considerably contracted where subdued or negative financial performance of the AIFM or of the AIF concerned occurs, taking into account both current compensation and reductions in pay-outs of amounts previously earned, including through malus or claw-back arrangements

Topic	Policy Requirements
Pension policy	-The pension policy is in line with the business strategy, objectives, values and long-term interests of the AIFM and the AIFs it manages -If the employee leaves the AIFM before retirement, discretionary pension benefits shall be held by the AIFM for a period of 5 years in the form of instruments -In the case of an employee reaching retirement, discretionary pension benefits shall be paid to the employee in the form of instruments subject to a 5 year retention period
Personal hedging strategies	-Staff should not use personal hedging strategies
Avoidance of AIFMD rules	-No compensation instruments should be used to circumvent the rules

5.4.2) Remuneration and Commission Recommendation 2009/384/EC:

The document sets out general principles applicable to remuneration practices in the financial services sector and aims at avoiding excessive risk-taking in the financial industry, especially by banks and investment firms. It applies to financial undertakings having their registered office or their head office in the territory of a Member State and covers remuneration of those categories of staff whose professional activities have a material impact on the risk profile of the financial undertaking. It does not apply to fees and commissions received by intermediaries and external service providers for delegated tasks and activities. Commission Recommendation 2009/384/EC requires the implementation of three overarching framework elements, which are:

(i)   the introduction of remuneration policy,

(ii)   the disclosure of remuneration information,

(iii)   and the supervision with regard to remuneration.

The remuneration policy must be in line with the business strategy, objectives and long-term interests of the company. It must offer a balance between fixed and variable components. Generally the fixed part should represent a significantly high proportion of the total remuneration. The policy must be regularly updated to ensure correspondence with company development. As part of the remuneration policy, the Supervisory Function must define general remuneration principles and control functions; human resources departments and external experts should also take an active role in the policy definition process. It must be subject to independent review at least on an annual basis.

Information on the remuneration policy must be disclosed periodically and should contain:

(i)   information on the decision-making process which
        defines the remuneration policy chosen;

(ii)   information on linkage between pay and performance;

(iii)   performance measurement criteria;

(iv)   the performance criteria on which the entitlement to
        shares, options or variable components of remunera-
        tion is based;

(v)   the main parameters and rationale for any annual bonus
        scheme and any other non-cash benefits

Competent Authorities shall carry out the supervisory activities
by taking into account the size of the financial undertaking, the
nature of its activities and the complexity of its activities. Financial undertakings should send to Competent Authorities a statement indicating the level of compliance with the principles of
Commission Recommendation 2009/384/EC.

5.4.3) ESMA Guidance on sound remuneration for AIFMs:

ESMA's guidance on remuneration for alternative investment
fund managers seems to be a logical next step in detailing out
remuneration rules. Before the financial crisis, it was especially
the remuneration practice in the hedge fund industry which
caught the attention of the public and the regulators. According to
a survey undertaken by the US business magazine Forbes in the

year 2013, the 25 highest-earning hedge fund managers together made about 24.3 billion USD, which is close to a billion each. Consequently, it seems justifiable to install additional mechanisms which help to ensure that the pay of the manager is not going to adversely affect the investors, especially in this very specific bucket of the financial industry.

For ESMA, remuneration consists of all possible forms of payments and benefits transferred by the AIFM to the benefit of the relevant staff categories. This includes:

(i)   any amount paid by the AIF including carried interest;

(ii)   any transfer of units or shares of the AIF;

(iii) co-investment arrangements funded by loans from the AIF which remain unpaid.

Not included are:

(i)   reimbursements of costs and expenses;

(ii)   dividends or similar distributions to employee shareholders or partners of AIFMs if not designed to circumvent the rules;

(iii) payment by the AIF which is a pro rata return on any investment made by a relevant staff member

ESMA extends the application of remuneration rules to delegates in the area of risk and portfolio management. To be compliant with AIFMD remuneration provisions the AIFM must ensure that the delegate is either subject to equivalent rules or contractual arrangements are in place which avoid any circumvention. This might trigger difficult discussions for AIFMs that have delegated risk and portfolio management to financial companies outside the EU. ESMA acknowledges that under specific circumstances the applicability of its remuneration requirements might not be useful. Therefore a proportionality approach was introduced so that in exceptional cases, specific provisions might be completely dis-applied based on:

(i)   the AuMs the AIFM manages;

(ii)   the AIFM's internal organisation;

(iii)   the nature, the scope and the complexity of the AIFMs activities.

Disapplication is possible with regard to the requirements on the pay-out processes for identified staff, including:

(i)   the payment of variable remuneration in whatever form;

(ii)   retention periods;

(iii)   deferral requirements;

(iv)   ex-post incorporation of risk or claw-back require-ments and the requirement to establish a remuneration committee.

Another enhancement of AIFMD remuneration rules in relation to Commission Recommendation 2009/384/EC is the requirement for significant AIFMs to establish a remuneration committee. The ESMA guidance offers a list of elements, expressly non-exclusive, to be taken into account to determine whether or not a remuneration committee is required. These are:

(i)   whether the AIFM is listed or not;

(ii)   the legal structure of the AIFM;

(iii)   the number of employees of the AIFM;

(iv)   the AIFM's assets under management;

(v)   whether the AIFM is also a UCITS management company.

ESMA also formulates a series of requirements with regard to the composition of the remuneration committee. In order to operate independently from senior executives, the remuneration committee should comprise members of the supervisory function who do not perform executive functions, at least the majority of whom qualify as independent. The chairperson of the remuneration committee should be an independent, non-executive member. An appropriate number of the members of the remuneration committee should have sufficient expertise and professional experience concerning risk management and control activities. The remuneration committee should be encouraged to seek expert advice internally (e.g. from risk management) and externally. The chief executive officer should not take part in the remuneration committee meetings when discussing or making decisions on his/her remuneration.

ESMA's guidance stipulates that an AIFM must prove that it has assessed and selected 'identified staff', defined as categories of staff including senior management, risk takers and control functions. This also includes

(i) any employee receiving total remuneration that takes them into the same remuneration bracket as senior management

(ii) risk takers whose professional activities have a material impact on the AIFM's risk profile or the risk profiles of the AIF that it manages

(iii) categories of staff of the entity(ies) to which portfolio management or risk management activities have been delegated by the AIFM, whose professional activities have a material impact on the risk profiles of the AIFs that the AIFM manages.

AIFMs should have the flexibility to disclose the information mentioned in the Recommendation through an independent remuneration policy statement, a periodic disclosure in the annual report or any other form. In all cases, however, the AIFM should ensure that the disclosure is clear and easily understandable and accessible. It should disclose detailed information regarding remuneration policies and practices for members of staff whose professional activities have a material impact on the risk profile of the AIFs the AIFM manages. AIFMs should also provide general information about the basic characteristics of their AIFM-wide remuneration policies and practices. Remuneration disclosures can be made on a proportionate basis and the overall remuneration proportionality principle will apply to the type and amount of information disclosed. Small or non-complex AIFMs/AIFs should only be expected to provide some qualitative information and very basic quantitative information where appropriate. The disclosure should be published on at least an annual basis and as soon as practicable after the information becomes available.

5.5)   Fair treatment of investors:

5.5.1)   Payment of fees, commissions and other benefits:

Generally, AIFMs must act fairly and honestly towards AIFs and investors. They must ensure that they are not charged any undue costs. AIFMs are deemed to act fairly and honestly if the fees, commissions and non-monetary benefits meet certain conditions. All payments must be related to the AIFM activities listed in Annex I of the AIFMD. A distinction is made between fees or benefits in relation to AIFs and those in relation to third parties. According to Article 24 of Commission Delegated Regulation 231/2013, fees, commissions and other benefits received from or provided to AIFs which are managed by the AIFM are unproblematic. Obviously the EU legislators are more concerned about relationships with third parties, as these could potentially create greater disadvantages. Therefore a fee, commission or non-monetary benefit paid or provided to a third party, or a person acting on behalf of a third party, needs to fulfil some additional criteria if the AIFM still wants to be deemed as acting fairly:

(i)   the existence, the nature and the amount of the fee must be clearly disclosed to investors;

(ii)   where the amount cannot be ascertained, the calcula-
         tion method must be disclosed;

(iii)   the payment of the fee or commission must be de-
         signed to enhance the quality of the relevant service;

(iv)   the fees must be necessary for the provision of the rel-
         evant services and the AIFM must disclose further de-
         tails if requested by the investor

The AIFM shall ensure that its decision-making procedures and
its organisational structure ensure fair treatment of investors.

5.5.2)   Best execution:

AIFMs must implement policies and procedures for preventing
malpractice impacting market stability and integrity. Whenever
AIFMs buy or sell financial instruments or other assets for which
best execution is relevant, they shall take all reasonable steps to
obtain the best possible result for the AIFs they manage or the
investors in these AIFs, taking into account:

(i)   the price,

(ii)   the costs,

(iii)   the speed,

(iv)   the likelihood of execution and settlement,

(v)   and the size, nature or any other consideration relevant
        to the execution of the order.

To comply with these obligations, the AIFM should establish in
writing and implement an execution policy to allow AIFs and
their investors to obtain, for AIF orders, the best possible execution result. AIFMs should monitor the effectiveness of their

arrangements on a regular basis and must be in a position to demonstrate adherence to the best execution policy. Appropriate information on the policy must be made available at the investors' request.

5.5.3) Personal account dealing:

According to Article 63 of Commission Delegated Regulation 231/2013, AIFMs are required to implement a personal account dealing monitoring framework. Not all employees must necessarily be covered. The provision defines that only:

(i)   relevant persons,

(ii)   involved in activities,

(iii)   that may give rise to a conflict of interest,

(iv)   or who have access to insider information must be subject to such procedures

A relevant person in relation to an AIFM is a director, partner, manager or employee, or any other natural person whose services are placed under the control of the AIFM and who is involved in the provision of collective portfolio management services. This should limit the scope of personal account dealing monitoring to the senior management, employees of independent control functions and employees involved in collective portfolio management, as these staff categories have permanent access to sensitive information. Based on how the AIFM is organised, other staff categories might also be included. AIFMs must prevent such relevant persons or their family members or persons with a close link to the relevant person from entering into financial transactions if the transaction:

(i)   is subject to Article 2(1) of Directive 2003/6/EC on insider information;

(ii)   involves the misuse or improper disclosure of confidential information;

(iii) conflicts with an obligation of the AIFM under AIFMD

Employees must be trained on personal transaction restrictions, and they must promptly inform the AIFM about any such transaction. Alternatively, the AIFM might run a system which allows it to discover such transactions on its own. A record of each transaction must be kept, including the authorization or prohibition decision. PAD rules are not applicable for discretionary portfolios without prior communication of transactions to the owner. PAD rules are not applicable for transactions in UCITS or AIFs where the originator is not involved in the management.

6.0) Authorisation:

Directive	Title	Article/Paragraph
2011/61/EU	Directive on Alternative Investment Fund Managers	§17 (introduction) Article 3 Article 4 Article 7 Article 15 Article 37 Article 43
231/2013	COMMISSION DELEGATED REGULATION on exemptions, general operating conditions, depositaries, leverage, transparency and supervision	Article 2 Article 5 Article 110

–   AIFMs with AuMs below the 100 or 500 million EUR thresholds can use the lighter regime

–   Small AIFMs can decide to opt in to take full advantage of the rights granted under the AIFMD

–   Generally the authorisation covers management and marketing in the Home Member State

–   There are specific rules for managing and marketing in other Member States

–   Non-EU AIFMs need to conduct a Member State of Reference assessment

6.1)   Lighter regime:

6.1.1)   Conditions for using the lighter regime:

The AIFMD offers a lighter regime for AIFMs where the cumulative AuMs of AIFs under management are below a threshold of 100 million EUR. Also, AIFMs that only manage:

(i)   unleveraged AIFs,

(ii)   without redemption rights for investors during the first 5 years,

(iii)   with cumulative AuMs of AIFs under management below a threshold of 500 million EUR

can use the lighter regime. While such AIFMs are unlikely to develop significant consequences for financial stability individually, it still might be possible that in aggregation their activities create systemic risks. Consequently, those entities are not subject to full authorisation but they are subject to registration. Assets under management must be frequently monitored, including the anticipation of:

(i)   subscriptions,

(ii)   redemptions,

(iii)   capital draw-downs,

(iv)   and distributions.

to check whether the AIFM still falls below the defined thresholds. AuMs must be calculated in accordance with Commission Delegated Regulation 231/2013, Art. 2, which applies a clear structure to the calculation process. Competent Authorities must be immediately notified in case the thresholds are violated. If registered under the lighter regime, it is not possible to benefit from other rights under AIFMD unless opting in.

6.1.2)   Information to be provided to Competent Authorities:

The registration of AIFMs falling below the defined thresholds requires transmitting specific information on to Competent Authorities. First of all, the AIFM needs to confirm and prove its own identity and that of the AIFs managed by it. Also, the total value of AuMs calculated in accordance with Commission Delegated Regulation 231/2013, Art. 2, §1 must be disclosed. With regard to the AIFs, the AIFM must provide:

(i)   the offering documents;

(ii)   an extract or a general description of the investment strategy, including the industrial, geographical or other market or sector focus;

(iii)   a description of the borrowing and leverage policy;

(iv)   the main instruments the AIFs trade in, including a breakdown of financial instruments;

(v)   the markets the AIFs actively trade in;

(vi)   the diversification of the portfolio, including principal exposures and important concentrations

The information provided for registration purposes must be updated and re-submitted to the Competent Authorities on an annual basis.

6.1.3)   Opting in:

Commission Implementing Regulation 447/2013 defines under which conditions the AIFM can opt in to profit from all benefits offered by the AIFMD. Under Article 1 it is stipulated that the AIFM has to submit a full application to its Competent Authority following the procedures under the AIFMD and its implementation directive. The Competent Authority may dispense AIFMs from submitting all information and documents required under Article 7 of the AIFMD if information or documents have already been submitted for registration purposes and are still up to date.

6.2)   Regular authorisation:

6.2.1)   Authorisation of EU AIFMs:

The authorization of EU AIFMs covers the management of EU AIFs established in their Home Member State and marketing to professional investors. The AIFMD does not contain any rules on marketing to retail investors. This remains within the sphere of the Member States. They can allow the marketing of AIFs to retail investors and they are allowed to impose stricter requirements for the AIFMs or the AIFs if they feel it might be required.

Where a UCITS ManCo applies for an AIFM license the information and documentation which can be required by Competent Authorities is limited to the AIFM and the AIFs it manages. The AIFM has to submit information on:

(i)   the persons effectively conducting the AIFM business,

(ii)   the identity of the AIFM shareholders that have qualified holdings,

(iii)   the organisational structure,

(iv)   how to comply with applicable parts of the AIFMD Directive,

(v)   the remuneration policies,

(vi)   and delegation and sub-delegation arrangements.

With regard to the AIFs it manages, it is required to provide information on:

(i)   the investment strategies and underlying funds in the case of a fund of fund structure,

(ii)   the AIF's policies with regard to the use of leverage,

(iii)   the risk profiles of the AIFs it manages or plans to
         manage,

(iv)   the Member States and the third countries in which the
         AIFs are or will be established,

(v)   the master AIF if the AIF is a feeder AIF,

(vi)   the instruments of incorporation for each AIF the
         AIFM intends to manage,

(vii)   the arrangements with the depositary for each AIF,

(viii)   and the disclosures made towards the investors accord-
         ing to AIFMD Art. 23 / §1 (for details please see chap-
         ter 11).

6.2.2)   Authorisation of non-EU AIFMs:

Non-EU AIFMs intending to manage EU AIFs and/or to market
AIFs managed by them in the European Union require authorisation. Even if the intention is to manage them without marketing
them, there is still no way to avoid the application for authorisation. They do not need to comply with AIFMD chapter VI (rights
of the EU AIFMs to Market and Manage EU AIFs in the Union).
For non-EU AIFMs the authorisation process starts differently.
As they are established outside EU law there is no and cannot be
a Home Member State. Consequently, the first step is to identify
the Member State and the Competent Authority in charge of conducting the authorisation, which is then called the Member State
of Reference. The AIFMD foresees that a Member State of Reference (MoR) assessment must be conducted, which requires ap-
proval by the Competent Authorities. In case of disagreement

with the outcome, the Competent Authorities of different Member States can refer the case to ESMA (the MoR process will be explained in detail in section 6.2.3).

To enforce an effective supervision, cooperation agreements must have been established between the Competent Authorities of the Member State of Reference and the third-country supervisor. It is important that the third country not be listed as an Non-Cooperative Country by the Financial Action Task Force (FATF), which is an inter-governmental policy-making body established in 1989 by the Ministers of its Member jurisdictions whose objectives are to set standards and promote effective implementation of legal, regulatory and operational measures for combating money laundering, terrorist financing and other related threats to the integrity of the international financial system. Currently the FATF has 34 members including all larger EU Member States, the USA, China, India, Russia, Japan and South Korea. There are 6 countries which are listed as non-cooperative, namely:

(i)   Iran,

(ii)   North Korea,

(iii)   Algeria,

(iv)   Ecuador,

(v)   Indonesia,

(vi)   and Myanmar.

The third country where the non-EU AIFM is established must have signed an agreement with the Member State of Reference to comply with the OECD Model Tax. The agreement must confirm the compliance with Article 26 on the exchange of information between Competent Authorities with regard to the enforcement of local tax laws.

The AIFMD anticipated that potential conflicts between the AIFMD and third-country regulation might occur, and it therefore provides a mechanism to solve the conflict of applying EU and third-country law at the same time. If AIFMD rules are incompatible with third-country rules the non-EU AIFM has to follow, Competent Authorities can dispense with the AIFMD rules under the condition that:

(i)   it is impossible to comply with the AIFMD rule and the third-country rule at the same time;

(ii)   the law has the same regulatory purpose;

(iii)   it provides the same degree of investor protection as EU law;

(iv)   the non-EU AIFM complies with the third-country rule.

The non-EU AIFM must appoint a legal representative who is deemed to be the contact person for ESMA and the Competent Authorities in the EU. The legal representative has to execute the compliance function.

Information must be provided to the Competent Authorities on:

(i)   the persons effectively conducting the AIFM business;

(ii)   the identity of the AIFM shareholders that have qualified holdings;

(iii)   the organisational structure;

(iv)   how to comply with applicable parts of the AIFMD Directive;

(v)   the remuneration policies;

(vi)   delegation and sub-delegation arrangements.

So far the requirements are the same for EU and non-EU AIFMs. In addition, the non-EU AIFM must submit:

(i)   a justification of the Member State of Reference assessment containing information on the marketing strategy;

(ii)   a list of AIFM provisions which are incompatible with third-country rules;

(iii)   written evidence-based confirmation that third-country law provides the same level of investor protection;

(iv)   the name of the legal representative and where it is established.

The information on AIFs to be provided to the Competent Authorities is limited to the EU AIFs and the AIFs the AIFM manages by itself or plans to market with a passport. For those it must submit information on:

(i)   the investment strategies,

(ii)   the underlying funds in case of a fund of funds structure,

(iii)   the Member States and the third countries in which the AIFs are or will be established,

(iv)   the master AIF if the AIF is a feeder AIF,

(v)   the disclosures made towards the investors according to AIFMD Art. 23, §1,

(vi)   the policy with regard to the use of leverage,

(vii)   the risk profiles of the AIFs the AIFM manages or plans to manage,

(viii) the instruments of incorporation for each AIF the AIFM manages or intends to manage,

(ix)   and the arrangements with the depositary for each AIF.

6.3) The Member State of Reference assessment:

6.3.1) AIFMD rules on the MoR selection (Directive 2011/61/EU):

Case	Case Description	Rules
No. 1 Art. 37, §4a	Non-EU AIFMs intending to manage one or several EU AIFs established in the same Member State without marketing in the EU	· The MoR is the Member State the where the AIFs are managed and marketed
No. 2 Art. 37 §4b	Non-EU AIFMs intending to manage EU AIFs established in different Member States without marketing in the Union	· The Member State of Reference is where most of the AIFs are established Or · The Member State of Reference is where the largest amount of assets is managed
No. 3 Art. 37 §4c	Non-EU AIFMs intending to market only one EU AIF in just one Member State	· If the AIF is authorised in a Member State, either the Home Member State or the state where the AIF is marketed is the MoR · If the AIF is not authorised

Case	Case Description	Rules
		in a Member State, the state where the AIFM intends to market the AIF is the MoR
No. 4 Art. 37 §4e	Non-EU AIFMs intending to market only one EU AIF in different Member States	· If the AIF is authorised in a Member State, it is either the HMS of the AIF or the one of the Member State where the AIFM intends to market · If the AIF is not authorised in a Member State, it is the one of the Member State where the AIFM intends to market
No. 5 Art 37 §4g	Non-EU AIFMs intending to market several EU AIFs in different Member States	· If the AIFs are all authorised in the same Member State then their HMS is the AIFM's MoR · Alternatively it can be the Member State where the AIFM intends to market the AIFs · If the AIFs are not all registered in the same Member State the MoR is the state

Case	Case Description	Rules
		where the majority of AIFs is marketed
No. 6 Art. 37 §4h	Non-EU AIFMs intending to market several non-EU AIFs and EU AIFs in different member states	· The MoR is the Member State where most of the AIFs will be marketed
No. 7 Art. 37 §4d	Non-EU AIFMs intending to market just one non-EU AIF in only one Member State	· The MoR is the Member State where the non-EU AIF is marketed
No. 8 Art. 37 §4f	Non-EU AIFMs intending to market just one non-EU AIF in different Member States	The MoR is one of the Member States where the non-EU AIF is marketed

6.3.2)   Change of marketing strategy:

Generally the Member State of Reference assessment should not be affected by the AIFM's further business development; but if within the first two years since authorization the marketing strategy materially changes, this must be communicated to the Competent Authorities. The AIFM must justify the new marketing strategy. If this leads to a different result in the Member State of Reference assessment, the legal representative must also be established in the new Member State of Reference. If it emerges within two years after authorization that false statements have been made, the MoR needs to be re-assessed. The basis for the re-assessment must be the new marketing strategy.

6.3.3)   The rules of Commission Implementing Directive 448/2013:

In 2013 the European Commission worked out additional rules regarding the Member State of Reference assessment and introduced Directive 44/2013. The directive is rather short and has just one article, which defines additional information and documentation requirements with regard to specific cases, as shown in the table below.

Case No.	Case Description	Additional Rules of Directive 448/2013
No. 1 Art. 37, §4a and **No. 2** Art. 37 §4b	Non-EU AIFMs intending to manage EU AIFs without marketing in the Union	· Has to submit the request to determine its Member State of Reference in writing · The request shall list all the possible Member States of Reference and shall be addressed to each of the Competent Authorities of the Member States that are possible Member States of Reference

Case No.	Case Description	Additional Rules of directive 448/2013
No. 2 Art. 37 §4b	Non-EU AIFMs intending to manage EU AIFs established in different Member States without marketing in the Union	· Must provide information and documentation which indicates: (i) the Member States where the managed AIFs are established (ii) the Member States where assets are managed by the non-EU AIFM (iii) the amounts of assets under management of the non-EU AIFM in the different Member States
No. 3 Art. 37 §4c	Non-EU AIFMs intending to market only one EU AIF in just one Member State	· Must provide information and documentation which indicates: (i) the Member State where the AIF managed by the non-EU AIFM is established (ii) the Member States where the non-EU AIFM intends to market the AIF

| No. 4 Art. 37 §4e and No. 5 Art 37 §4g | Non-EU AIFMs intending to market only one EU AIF in different Member States and Non-EU AIFMs intending to market several EU AIFs in different Member States | · Must provide information and documentation which indicates the Member States where AIFs managed by a non-EU AIFM are established
· A description of the marketing strategy, indicating at least:
(i) the Member States where the distributors are going to promote the AIFs, including the expected AuM share
(ii) an estimate of the expected number of investors targeted having their domicile in the Member States where the AIFM intends to market its AIFs
(iii) the official languages of Member States into which the offering and promotional documents have been or are to be translated
(iv) the distribution of marketing activities across the Member States where the AIFM intends to market its AIFs, taking into account in particular the prominence and frequency of advertisements and road shows |

Case No.	Case Description	Additional Rules of directive 448/2013
No. 8 Art. 37 §4f	Non-EU AIFMs intending to market just one non-EU AIF in different Member States	• A description of the marketing strategy, indicating at least: (i) the Member States where the distributors are going to promote the AIFs, including the expected AuM share (ii) an estimate of the expected number of investors targeted having their domicile in the Member States where the AIFM intends to market its AIFs (iii) the official languages of Member States into which the offering and promotional documents have been or are to be translated (iv) the distribution of marketing activities across the Member States where the AIFM intends to market its AIFs, taking into account in particular the prominence and frequency of advertisements and road shows

7.0) Passporting regime:

Directive	Title	Article/Paragraph
2011/61/EU	Directive on Alternative Investment Fund Managers	§63 (introduction)
		§69 (introduction)
		Article 21
		Article 31
		Article 32
		Article 33
		Article 34
		Article 35
		Article 39
		Article 40
		Article 41
		Article 42
		Article 43
		Appendix III

– The authorisation base case for AIFMs covers managing and marketing in the Home Member State

– Managing and marketing outside the Home Member State requires registration

– All requests are handled via the Competent Authorities of the AIFM's Home Member State

– Competent Authorities have to respond no later than 20 days after filing the request

– The Competent Authorities of the Home Member State will inform the affected regulators

7.1)   Introduction to passporting:

Passporting is the process defined under the AIFMD whereby AIFMs have to notify the Competent Authorities of their Home Member State (EU AIFMs) or their Member State of Reference (non-EU AIFMs) about any extra activity not already covered by the AIFM's initial authorisation. The base case for the AIFMD authorisation granted by the Competent Authorities, regardless of whether an EU AIF or a non-EU AIFM applied for a licence, covers the management of AIFs in the AIFM's Home Member State or Member State of Reference. The marketing of EU AIFs in the Home Member State already requires registration with the Competent Authorities. The EU legislators attempted to strike a balance between obtaining information on the activities of AIFMs in

---

the Union and not imposing new administrative burdens on managers, which might have weakened the EU in comparison to other financial markets. Requests for marketing in other EU countries or for managing AIFs established in other Member States can be addressed to the Competent Authorities of the Home Member State or the Member State of Reference and a reply must be provided within 20 working days, ensuring the timeliness of responses. The information to be provided by AIFMs is defined in the AIFMD's Annex III for requests concerning EU AIFs and in Annex IV for requests concerning non-EU AIFs. Whenever the AIFM wants to pursue activities in relation to non-EU AIFs it must ensure that:

(i)   adequate cooperation agreements are in place between the AIFM's Competent Authorities and the supervisory authority of the non-EU AIF's country of incorporation;

(ii)   the country is not listed by the FATF as non-cooperative;

(iii)   adherence to Article 26 of the OECD Model Tax Convention is given.

As the whole AIFMD passporting section is not designed in a very efficient manner, there is a lot of duplication. To provide an overview of all the different requirement variations, I explain every case in detail in the following sections.

7.2) Passporting for EU AIFMs:

7.2.1) Passporting for EU AIFs:

7.2.1.1) Passport for managing AIFs established in another Member State:

EU AIFMs can manage EU AIFs established in Member States other than their Home Member State if they adhere to the conditions of the AIFMD's Article 33. It stipulates that the AIFM can either manage directly or via a branch. The EU AIFM must send a notification to the Competent Authorities for each EU AIF that it intends to manage. The information to be sent to the Competent Authorities covers:

(i)   the organisational structure of the branch;

(ii)   the address of the AIF in its HMS;

(iii)   the programme of operations to be conducted by the AIFM for the specific AIF.

Material changes with regard to the initial facts communicated must be submitted to the Competent Authorities one month before they take effect. If planned changes are implemented against the recommendation of the Competent Authorities, the AIFM's right to market those AIFs may be withdrawn.

7.2.1.2) Passport for marketing in the AIFM's Home Member State:

EU AIFs can market AIFs in their HMS if they adhere to the conditions of the AIFMD's Article 31. The EU AIFM must send a notification to the Competent Authorities for each EU AIF. The EU AIFM must adhere to minimum content requirements with regard to the notification described in the AIFMD, Annex III. The AIFM must send:

(i)   a notification letter, including a programme of operations identifying the AIFs the AIFM intends to market and information on where the AIFs are established;

(ii)   the AIF rules or instruments of incorporation;

(iii) the identification of the depositary of the AIF;

(iv)   a description of the information on the AIF available to investors;

(v)   information on where the master AIF is established if the AIF is a feeder AIF;

(vi)   any additional information referred to in the AIFMD's Article 23, §1 (explained in detail in chapter 11) for each AIF the AIFM intends to market;

(vii) where relevant, information on the arrangements established to prevent units or shares of the AIF from being marketed to retail investors, including in the case where the AIFM relies on the activities of independent entities to provide investment services for the AIF.

The earliest point in time to start the marketing activities is when the AIFM receives the acknowledgement letter from the Competent Authorities. Material changes to initially communicated facts must be submitted to the Competent Authorities one month before their effectiveness. If planned changes are implemented against the recommendation of the Competent Authorities, the AIFM's right to market those AIFs may be withdrawn.

7.2.1.3) Passporting for marketing in other Member States:

EU AIFMs can market EU AIFs in other Member States if they adhere to the conditions of the AIFMD's Article 32. It requires the AIFM to send a notification to the Competent Authorities for each EU AIF it intends to market in another Member State. The EU AIFM must adhere to minimum content requirements with regard to the notification, as defined in the AIFMD's Annex IV. The contents of the notification letter as defined in Annex IV is identical to the contents of the notification letter as defined in Annex III and was already described in section 7.1.1.2. The only addition is that the AIFM has to indicate the Member State in which it intends to market the units or shares of the AIF to professional investors. The earliest point in time to start the marketing activities is when the AIFM receives the acknowledgement letter from the Competent Authorities. Material changes to the initially communicated facts must be submitted to the Competent Authorities one month before they take effect. If planned changes are implemented against the recommendation of the Competent Authorities, the AIFM's right to market those AIFs may be withdrawn.

7.2.2)   Passporting for non-EU AIFs:

7.2.2.1) Passport for managing non-EU AIFs:

In this specific case, the AIFMD remains a bit unclear about the exact requirements. Article 34 only states that the AIFM must adhere to all AIFMD requirements with the exception of Article 21 (Depositary Requirements) and Article 22 (Annual Report) with regard to the non-EU AIFs it intends to manage. In addition, it stipulates that adequate cooperation agreements must be in place between the Competent Authority of the AIFM's Home Member State and the supervision body of the non-EU AIF. The question is now whether the AIFM must send a notification letter to the Competent Authorities with the content described in Annex III or Annex IV. Some interpretation might be required here. The origin and the purpose of the AIFMD framework is:

(i)   investor protection;

(ii)   conservation or enhancement of the integrity of finan-cial markets;

(iii) prevention of systemic risk which might trigger a breakdown of the financial system.

Therefore it is recommended to notify the Competent Authorities of the AIFM's Home Member State about every new non-EU AIF the AIFM intends to manage.

7.2.2.2) Passport for marketing non-EU AIFs in the Union:

EU AIFMs can market non-EU AIFs in their Home Member State or in other Member States of the Union, as long as they ad-here to the conditions of the AIFMD's Article 33. AIFMs must comply with all requirements of the AIFMD except chapter VI (Right of the EU AIFMs to market and to manage EU AIFs in the Union). Adequate cooperation agreements must be in place be-tween the Competent Authorities of the AIFM's Home Member

State and the supervision body of the non-EU AIF. The third country where the non-EU AIF is established should not be listed as a Non-Cooperative Country and Territory by the FATF (please see section 6.1.2 for information on FATF). An agreement must be in place between the third country and the AIFM's Home Member State to comply with Art. 26 of the OECD Model Tax Convention (please see section 6.1.2 for information on Article 26 of the OECD Model Tax Convention). The EU AIFM must send a notification to the Competent Authorities of its Home Member State for each non-EU AIF it intends to market in the Union. If the marketing is only planned in the AIFM's Home Member State the content of the notification is defined by Annex III. If the marketing is also planned in other Member States, the content of the notification is defined in Annex IV.

7.3) Passporting for non-EU AIFMs:

7.3.1) Passporting for EU AIFs:

7.3.1.1) Managing AIFs established in another Member State:

Non-EU AIFMs are allowed to manage EU AIFs established in another Member State, which is not their Member State of Reference, if they adhere to the conditions of the AIFMD's Article 41. The AIFM can decide to either manage directly or through a branch. The EU AIFM must send a notification to the Competent Authorities for each EU AIF it intends to manage. The notification letter should contain:

(i)   the Member State in which it plans to manage the non-EU AIFMs;

(ii)   whether it plans to manage directly or through a branch;

(iii)   the programme of operations.

If it plans to manage through a branch, it must supplement the notification with:

(i)   the organisational structure of the branch;

(ii)   the address of AIFs in the Member state of Reference;

(iii)   the responsible persons.

The earliest point in time to start with the marketing activities is when the AIFM receives the acknowledgement from the Competent Authorities. Material changes to the facts initially communicated must be submitted to the Competent Authorities one month before they take effect. If it implements planned changes against the recommendation of the Competent Authorities, the AIFM's right to market those AIFs may be withdrawn.

7.3.1.2) *Marketing of EU AIFs in the Union:*

Non-EU AIFMs can market EU AIFs in their Member State of Reference or other Member States if they adhere to the conditions of the AIFMD's Article 39. They are required to send a notification to the Competent Authorities for each EUAIF they intend to market. The non-EU AIFM must adhere to minimum content requirements with regard to the notification as defined in the AIFMD's Annex III if it plans to market in its Member State of Reference and Annex IV if it intends to market in another

Member State. The contents of the notification letter as defined in Annex IV are identical to the contents of the notification letter as defined in Annex III and were already described in section 7.2.1.2. The only addition is that the AIFM has to indicate the Member State in which it intends to market the units or shares of the AIF to professional investors. The earliest point in time to start the marketing activities is when the AIFM receives the acknowledgement letter from the Competent Authorities. Material changes to the initially communicated facts must be submitted to the Competent Authorities one month before they take effect. If it implements planned changes against the recommendation of the Competent Authorities, the AIFM's right to market those AIFs may be withdrawn.

7.3.2) Passporting for non-EU AIFs:

7.3.2.1) Marketing of non-EU AIFs in the Union:

Non-EU AIFMs can market non-EU AIFs in their Home Member State or other Member States of the Union so long as they adhere to the conditions of the AIFMD's Article 40. AIFMs must comply with all requirements of the AIFMD except chapter VI (Right of the EU AIFMs to market and to manage EU AIFs in the Union). Adequate cooperation agreements must be in place between the Competent Authorities of the AIFM's Home Member State and the supervision body of the non-EU AIF. The third country where the non-EU AIF is established should not be listed as a Non-Cooperative Country and Territory by the FATF (please see section 6.1.2 for information on FATF). An agreement must be in place between the third country and the AIFM's Home Member State to comply with Art. 26 of the OECD Model Tax Convention (please see section 6.1.2 for information on Article 26 of the OECD Model Tax Convention). The EU AIFM must send a notification to the Competent Authorities of its Home Member State for each non-EU AIF it intends to market in the Union. If the marketing is only planned in the AIFM's Home Member State the contents of the notification are defined by Annex III. If the marketing is also planned in other Member States, the contents of the notification are defined in Annex IV.

7.4)   Private placement regime:

Currently EU AIFMs managing EU AIFs have the advantage of being in a position to use the passporting regime when expanding their business to other Member States. For non-EU AIFMs the passport will not be available for EU AIFs or non-EU AIFs managed by them until 2016. Since 22 July 2014, non-EU AIFMs have to comply with national private placement regimes introduced under the AIFMD when marketing such AIFs in the Union. They are implemented on a country-by-country basis. The AIFMD introduces minimum standards, but Member States can decide to impose stricter rules if they feel this is required. Non-EU AIFMs planning to manage EU AIFs must comply with all AIFMD requirements with the exception of the depositary requirements. One or more entities must be appointed to carry

out the depositary tasks. With regard to non-EU AIFs, the requirements for disclosure to investors must be similar to those
applicable to EU AIFMs managing EU AIFs. Non-EU AIFMs
must also adhere to this directive's requirements on reporting to
the

Competent Authorities and requirements with regard to acquiring
control over non-listed companies and issuers.

8.0) Appointment of the depositary:

Directive	Title	Article/Paragraph
2011/61/EU	Directive on Alternative Investment Fund Managers	Article 21 Article 34 Article 35 Article 43
231/2013	COMMISSION DELE-GATED REGULATION on exemptions, general operating conditions, de-positaries, leverage, trans-parency and supervision	Article 83 Article 84
2009/65/EC	Directive on the coordina-tion of laws, regulations and administrative provi-sions relating to undertak-ings for collective invest-ment in transferable securi-ties (UCITS)	Article 23

- A single depositary must be appointed for each AIF to be evidenced by a written contract
- The depositary must be authorised in the EU to provide depositary services
- For real estate, infrastructure and private equity funds a notary can be the depositary
- The AIFMD lists some entities which should not act as depositaries
- There are detailed requirements with regard to the content of the contract with the depositary

8.1) Entities accepted as a depositary:

The AIFM must appoint a single depositary for each AIF it manages. This must be evidenced by a written contract. The minimum content requirements are defined in Commission Delegated Regulation 231/2013 Article 83, No. 1a –r. There is no need to enter into an agreement for every single AIF; a master agreement is sufficient. Generally, information flows between involved parties can be of an electronic nature if proper record-keeping is in place. The AIFMD defines exactly who can act as a depositary for AIF assets and it also regulates in detail where the depositary must be incorporated or where it is required to have or to establish a branch for conducting business.

An investment firm with registered office in the European Union can act as a depositary if:

(i)   it is subject to capital adequacy requirements in accordance with Article 20(1) of Directive 2006/49/EC (capital adequacy of investment firms and credit institutions);

(ii)   it is subject to capital requirements for operational risks and is authorised in accordance with Directive 2004/39/EC (markets in financial instruments);

(iii)   it provides the ancillary service of safe-keeping and administration of financial instruments for the account of clients in accordance Directive 2004/39/EC;

(iv)   it has own funds not less than the amount of initial capital referred to in Article 9 of Directive 2006/49/EC.

Credit Institutions are also allowed to act as a depositary. They must have their registered office in the European Union and authorisation in accordance with Directive 2006/48/EC (taking up and pursuit of the business of credit institutions) must be given. The AIFMD refers to UCITS Directive 2009/65/EC, which lists condition under which Member States can allow other financial institutions to act as a depositary under Article 23, §3 of the Directive. According to this definition a depositary can also be an institution which is subject to prudential regulation and ongoing supervision with sufficient financial and professional guarantees to be able to effectively pursue its business as a depositary. Consequently, Member States might allow notaries, lawyers, registrars or another entity to act as depositary for AIF assets. For AIFs that generally do not invest in assets to be held in custody, a notary, a lawyer or a registrar can be the depositary under the condition that the AIF does not grant redemption rights for the first 5 years. Additionally, the appointed entity must be subject to mandatory professional registration by law or to legal or regulatory provisions. The appointed entity must be able to provide adequate capital or professional guarantees.

For non-EU AIFs, and only for them, there is the possibility for the depositary to be a non-EU-licensed credit institution or any other entity of the same nature if it is subject to effective prudential regulation and supervision.

8.2)   Entities which should not act as a depositary:

To avoid conflicts of interest between the AIFM and the AIF, the AIFM itself should generally not act as a depositary. Prime brokers can, but they must adhere to specific rules. If they also act as counterparty to one or more AIFs managed by the AIFM, they shall not act as depositaries unless the depositary function is adequately separated from other functions of their business (for requirements with regard to functional and hierarchical separation please see Commission Delegated Regulation 231/2013, Article 42). Conflicts of interest must be properly identified, managed, monitored and disclosed to investors.

8.3)   Location of the depositary:

As a general rule, under the AIFMD the depositary should have its registered office or a branch in the country where the AIF is established. With regard to EU AIFs, it should be incorporated in the AIF's Home Member State.

Different requirements exist for non-EU AIFs; the depositary should be established either:

(i)   in the third country where the AIF is established;

(ii)   in the Home Member State of the AIFM;

(iii)   or in the Member State of Reference of the AIFM.

Under certain conditions, third-country depositaries can be appointed. This requires that cooperation agreements must be in place between the Competent Authorities of the depositary and the country where the AIF will be marketed. The depositary also must be subject to prudential regulation, including minimal capital requirements and supervision which has the same effect as Union law. The third country should not be listed as a Non-Cooperative Country or Territory by the FATF and it must fully comply with Article 26 of the OECD Model Tax Convention. The depositary shall by contract be liable to the AIF or to the investors. Whenever the depositary is based in a third country the adequacy of the regulation and authorisation must be assessed. According to Article 84 of Commission Delegated Regulation 231/2013, the depositary must be subject to authorisation and ongoing supervision by a competent public authority which is equipped with adequate resources. The law of the third country must lay down objective criteria for obtaining an authorisation as a depositary which should have the same effect as the laws for access to the business of credit institutions or investment firms within the European Union. Third-country capital requirements, depositary operating conditions and requirements regarding the specific duties of AIF depositaries in the third country must also have the same effect as Union law.

8.4)   Contract with the depositary:

At a minimum, the contract between the AIFM and the depositary must contain:

(i)   a description of the services to be provided by the depositary;

(ii)   a description of the way in which the safe-keeping and oversight function is to be performed;

(iii)   a statement that the depositary's liability shall not be affected by any delegation of its custody functions (under specific conditions described in Article 21, §§ 13, 14 a discharge is possible);

(iv)   the period of validity;

(v)   the conditions for amendment and termination of the contract;

(vi)   confidentiality obligations;

(vii)   the means and procedures used to exchange relevant information;

(viii) the conditions for the re-use of the assets;

(ix)   the procedures to be followed when an amendment to the AIF rules, instruments of incorporation or offering documents is being considered;

(x)   the necessary information to be exchanged between the involved parties (AIF, AIFM, depositary and delegates);

(xi)   a commitment to provide, on a regular basis, details of any third party appointed;

(xii)   the tasks and responsibilities relating to the prevention of money laundering and the financing of terrorism;

(xiii) information on all cash accounts opened in the name of the AIF or in the name of the AIFM;

(xiv)   details regarding the depositary's escalation procedures;

(xv)   a commitment by the depositary to notify the AIFM when it becomes aware that the segregation of assets is no longer sufficient;

(xvi)   the procedures ensuring that the depositary can enquire into the conduct of the AIF and the AIFM;

(xvii) the procedures ensuring that the AIFM and the AIF can review the performance of the depositary.

9.0) Risk management:

Directive	Title	Article/Paragraph
2011/61/EU	Directive on Alternative Investment Fund Managers	Article 15
		Article 16
231/2013	COMMISSION DELE-GATED REGULATION on exemptions, general operating conditions, depositaries, leverage, transparency and supervision	Article 13
		Article 18
		Article 19
		Article 20
		Article 39
		Article 40
		Article 41
		Article 42
		Article 43
		Article 44
		Article 45
		Article 46
		Article 47
		Article 48
		Article 51
		Article 52
		Article 53
		Article 55

–   AIFMs must establish an independent risk management function including a risk management policy

–   The risk management function must be functionally and hierarchically separated

–   The risk management policy must cover market risk, liquidity risk, counterparty risk and operational risk

–   The AIFM must establish risk limits for all risk categories and it must monitor adherence

–   There are extensive due diligence requirements with regards to securitisation positions

9.1)   Establishing the risk management function:

AIFMs must implement a risk management system to identify, measure, manage and monitor all risks. The risk management system is defined as:

(i)   the AIFM's organisational structure;

(ii)   the permanent risk management function;

(iii)   policies and procedures;

(iv)   tools to measure risk.

The risk management function must be equipped with the necessary authority. The AIFM must implement sound risk management policy and procedures which help to ensure that the risk profile of the AIFs it manages stay in line with the defined risk limits. Those risk limits must be permanently monitored and the risk function must inform the governing body and the supervisory function in a timely manner in case of any breaches.

The governing body and the supervisory function should receive regular updates on:

(i)   the compliance with risk limits;

(ii)   the effectiveness of the risk management function;

(iii) the current level of risk incurred by each AIF.

Regarding the contents, the risk management policy must cover market risk, liquidity risk, counterparty risk and operational risk. It should describe:

(i)   the techniques, the tools and other arrangements for all the previously mentioned risk categories;

(ii)   the roles & responsibilities with regard to risk management;

(iii) the quantitative and qualitative risk limits set in accordance with Commission Delegated Regulation 231/2013, Article 44;

(iv)   terms, content, frequency and the addressees of the reporting provided by the risk management function;

(v)   potential conflicts of interests and remedial measures.

With regard to the risk management function, the governing body or the supervisory function must implement safeguards against potential conflicts of interest. These safeguards include that:

(i)   decisions of the risk management function must be based on reliable data;

(ii)   the remuneration of risk management function em-
         ployees is independent of the performance of the busi-
         ness areas;

(iii)   the risk management function is subject to independent
         review to ensure that decisions are made independent-
         ly,

(iv)   the risk management function is represented in the
         governing body or the supervisory function;

(v)   conflicting duties are clearly separated;

(vi)   the risk management function is frequently reviewed
         by the internal audit function;

(vii)   where a risk committee is established, non-independent
         members should not have undue influence.

9.2)   Operational risk:

The operational risk management must be performed independently as part of the risk management function. The AIFM
must implement well-documented operational risk management
policies and procedures and must ensure compliance with those
documents. In case of non-compliance, it must take adequate and
timely actions. The operational risk policy must be reviewed at
least annually. The AIFM must set up a historical loss database
and ensure the capture of:

(i)   operational failures,

(ii)   loss experience,

(iii)   damage experience,

(iv)   and liability risk.

The risk framework should make use of:

(i)   internal events,

(ii)   external events,

(iii)   scenario analysis,

(iv)   and the business environment and control factors.

Operational risk exposure and loss experience must be monitored on an ongoing basis and should be subject to regular reporting to the governing body and the supervisory function.

9.3)   Liquidity risk management:

AIFMs must establish a liquidity risk management system for all AIFs they manage, with the exception of unleveraged closed-ended AIFs. The main target of the liquidity risk management is to ensure that the investment strategy, the liquidity profile and the redemption policy are consistent. The AIFM must be able to demonstrate to the Competent Authorities that such a system is in place and it must be documented in the form of policies or procedures, which need to be reviewed at least annually. A minimum level of liquidity must be maintained for all AIFs. The level must be adequate in relation to the assets held by the AIF and the time required to liquidate them. In addition, AIFMs are required to establish liquidity or illiquidity limits and compliance with these limits must be frequently monitored. In the case of current or predicted limit infringements, the course of action to avoid breaches must be defined. AIFMs have to monitor the AIF liquidity profile, including the marginal contribution of individual assets which might impact the overall liquidity profile. The AIFMs should also take into account the impact of redemptions on liquidity by considering:

(i)   the investor basis,

(ii)   the relative size of investments,

(iii)   and the redemption terms.

If the AIF invests in other collective investment undertakings, the AIFM must periodically review their liquidity management. If the collective investment undertakings trade in regulated markets the review of liquidity management is not required. The AIFM must assess the quantitative and qualitative risks of current positions and intended investments. The AIFM must have appropriate knowledge of the liquidity of current positions or intended investments. The AIFM must regularly conduct stress tests under normal and exceptional conditions. Stress tests must be based on reliable data. They should simulate a shortage of liquidity and atypical redemptions and must include consequential impacts including margin calls, collateral requirements and credit lines. They should also consider valuation sensitivities under stressed conditions. Escalation procedures must be in place to be applied in case of anticipated or actual liquidity shortages.

9.4)   Securitisation positions:

Financial markets have many types of securitisation positions. One of the most famous types since the US subprime crisis is mortgage-backed securities, which is when banks put a number of loans they want to get rid of into a special purpose legal entity which is then sold to investors. Before the breakout of the subprime crisis and the disastrous decline in value, financial institutions around the world bought all kinds of securitised loans without proper initial and ongoing due diligence. As a consequence, even financially sound corporations were close to bankruptcy and governments had to provide billions of additional equity to bail them out. The role of Alternative Investment Funds in the subprime crisis is not completely clear, and there are divergent opinions. The fact is that they were not involved in the loan packaging and selling process. According to a newspaper article published in the British *Financial Times*[8] at end of 2006, hedge funds held around 47 per cent of the 3 trillion USD Collateralised Debt Obligations (CDO) market. The EU legislators applied the lessons learned from the financial crisis when designing the Alternative Fund Managers Directive. The AIFMD establishes a strict framework for alternative fund managers in case they want to invest in any kind of securitised positions. As the rules are quite extensive, the question arises whether the framework leads to quasi-prohibition of such positions in the alternative investments area. The AIFMD requires the AIFM to execute an initial due diligence on the originator, whereby it needs to determine whether the originator:

---

[8] UK Financial Times, 01/04/2012, written by Photis Lysandrou

(i)   issues credits according to well defined criteria;

(ii)   has policies in place for approving, amending and re-
        viewing credits, and has effective systems in place to
        administer the loan portfolio and to identify problem
        loans;

(iii)   has an adequately diversified credit portfolio;

(iv)   has a written credit policy in place including risk limits
        and monitoring controls;

(v)   grants access to all documents on credit quality and the
        performance of individual loans and other information;

(vi)   discloses the levels of retained net economic interests.

AIFMs may only invest on behalf of AIFs in securitisation positions if the originator retains a material net economic interest,
which should at all times be no less than 5% of the nominal value
of all tranches sold to investors. The original lender must explicit-
ly disclose to the AIFM that it retains this level. The net economic exposure is measured at origination and it should not be subject
to credit risk mitigation, to short positions or to any other hedge.
The net economic interest is not required if a guarantee is issued
by institutions listed in Article 122a, §3 of Directive 2006/48/EC
(this must be a mistake in the AIFMD, as there is no Article 122a
in Directive 2006/48/EC). In addition to the checks on the issuer,
due diligence must be performed on the individual securities.
AIFMs must be able to demonstrate that they have policies and
procedures in place with regard to analysing these positions. The
AIFM must check, initially and on an ongoing basis:

(i)   the retained net economic interest,

(ii)   the risk characteristics of the individual position,

(iii)   the risk characteristics of the underlying exposures,

(iv)   the reputation and the loss experience of the originator
        in earlier securitisations,

(v)   the statements made by the originator with regard to its
        due diligence on the exposures and collateral,

(vi)   and the structural features of the individual positions.

Where the AIFM entered into material credit risk exposure through securitisation positions, regular stress testing is required. For all securitisation positions, formal credit risk monitoring must be introduced, covering any kind of credit risk-related data. In case the underlying exposures themselves are securitisation positions, a complete examination is required.

The rules must be applied to all securitisation positions issued after 01/01/2011 and to all existing securitisation positions after 31/12/2014.

9.5)   Mandatory checks and reviews:

AIFMs must implement qualitative and quantitative risk limits for market, credit, liquidity, counterparty and operational risk for each AIF they manage. The limits must be aligned with the over-all risk profile of the individual AIF. If the AIFM decides to just implement qualitative risk limits, it needs to explain this decision to the Competent Authorities. AIFMs are required to identify, measure, manage and monitor the risk of each AIF. The risk of individual positions and their contribution to the overall risk profile must be measured. Periodically, the AIFMs must execute back testing, including model-based forecasts, and stress testing, including scenario analysis, to address the risk of changing market conditions. They must ensure that the current level of risk is in line with the defined risk limits. Escalation procedures must be in place to address current or anticipated breaches of those risk limits.

The AIFMD requires that the risk management system be reviewed on a regular basis and that in some specific instance reviews be triggered by events. Generally, the frequency of these reviews has to be defined by the AIFM's senior management, but they should be carried out at least annually. They are required to assess:

(i)   the effectiveness of the risk management policy;

(ii)   the degree of compliance with the risk management policy;

(iii)   the effectiveness of addressing deficiencies;

(iv)   the performance of the risk management function;

(v)   the effectiveness of the functional and hierarchical separation of the risk management function.

Instant reviews are required whenever:

(i)   material changes to the risk policy occur;

(ii)   there are material internal or external events;

(iii)   there are material changes with regard to the investment strategy, which also requires informing the Competent Authorities.

When selecting prime brokers, due diligence must be performed. Additional checks are required if the prime broker is meant to carry out OTC derivatives, securities lending or re-purchase agreement transactions. This requires that the prime broker:

(i)   is subject to supervision,

(ii)   is financially sound,

(iii)   has sufficient organisational structures in place,

(iv)   and is subject to prudential regulation.

The list of approved prime brokers must be signed off by the AIFM's senior management.

AIFMs must establish and apply written investment due diligence policies and procedures. These must be regularly reviewed and updated. If investing in assets of limited liquidity, a business plan must be developed which is in line with the AIF's duration and a complete due diligence must be performed on such investments. The AIMF is also required to monitor the performance of the investment in comparison with the business plan. All records must be retained for at least 5 years.

10.0) Acquiring control over companies:

Directive	Title	Article/Paragraph
2011/61/EU	Directive on Alternative Investment Fund Managers	§53 (introduction Article 27 Article 28 Article 29 Article 30

Key requirements:

–   AIFMs acquiring shares in non-listed companies must inform the Competent Authorities

–   There are specific thresholds which trigger the notification

–   When taking over control, the AIFM must also inform the board and employees of that company

–   The notification should take place no later than 10 days after acquisition

–   The AIFM is not allowed to conduct any capital reducing measures within the first two years

10.1) Notification and disclosure requirements:

Disclosures regarding takeovers in regulated markets must be in line with 2004/25/EC and 2004/109/EC. Specific requirements have to be applied with regard to acquiring control of non-listed companies. Whenever the AIF's holding of shares in non-listed companies changes, the AIFM must inform the Competent Authorities if specific thresholds are exceeded. If it acquires control, the AIFM must also notify the acquired company, its shareholders and the Competent Authorities. The notification shall contain information on:

(i)   the voting rights situation after acquisition;

(ii)   the date control was acquired;

(iii)   the identity of the purchaser;

(iv)   the conditions of the acquisition.

In the notification letter, the AIFM should request that the management of the acquired company informs the employees or their representatives. The notification should happen as soon as possible, without any undue delay, but no later than 10 days after acquiring control. When acquiring control over non-listed companies, specific information must be made available without any undue delay to the company itself, to its shareholders, to employees and their representatives and to the Competent Authorities. The AIFM must disclose its intentions with regard to the future business of the non-listed company and the likely repercussions on employment, including any material change in the conditions of employment. Information on how the deal was financed must be provided to the AIF's investors. The annual report of the acquired company must be made available by the management of that company to its employees. A review of the development of the acquired company and information on the likely future development must be included in the AIF's or the acquired company's annual report.

10.2) Prohibition on capital reductions:

Within 24 months after acquiring control, the AIFM is prohibited from ordering distributions, capital reductions, share redemption or purchases or any other kind of capital reducing measures. Distributions are defined as payments of dividends and of interests relating to shares and they are prohibited when the net assets fall below the subscribed capital plus non-distributable reserves or when they exceed the earnings of the last financial year. The acquisition of own shares is prohibited if the net assets fall below the subscribed capital plus the non-distributable reserve. Reductions in the subscribed capital are allowed to cover losses and to put money in a non-distributable reserve.

11.0) Reporting and mandatory documents:

Directive	Title	Article/Paragraph
2011/61/EU	Directive on Alternative Investment Fund Managers	§48 (introduction)
		Article 9
		Article 21
		Article 22
		Article 23
		Article 24
231/2013	COMMISSION DELE-GATED REGULATION on exemptions, general operating conditions, depositaries, leverage, transparency and supervision	Article 6
		Article 7
		Article 8
		Article 11
		Article 104
		Article 108
		Article 109
		Article 110

– AIFMs must provide an annual report for each AIF they manage or market in the Union

– The AIFMD defines the basic structure and the minimum contents of the report

– Specific information must be provided to investors before investing in an AIF (prospectus)

– The AIFMD requires that AIFMs must disclose certain additional information periodically to investors

– Specific information must be provided to the Competent Authorities at least on an annual basis

11.1) Annual report:

For each EU AIF they manage or for each AIF they market in the European Union, AIFMs must provide an annual report no later than 6 months after the end of the financial year. The report must be made available to the Competent Authorities of the AIFM and the AIF Home Member State and to investors upon request. Whenever an AIF trades in regulated markets the annual report must be provided no later than 4 months after the end of the financial year and should be in line with Directive 2004/109/EC (harmonisation of transparency requirements in relation to information about issuers whose securities are admitted to trading on a regulated market). Only the AIFMD's Article 22, §2, which defines minimum content requirements for the annual report, additionally applies. At a minimum, the annual report must contain:

(i)   a balance sheet;

(ii)   an income and expenditure account;

(iii)   a description of the AIF's activities;

(iv)   a description of any material changes with regard to the accounting standard;

(v)   the total amount of remuneration split into fixed and variable parts paid to AIFM staff;

(vi)   the number of staff;

(vii)   the total amount of remuneration broken down by payments made to senior management and staff impacting the AIF risk profiles;

(viii) the remuneration and staff of the AIFM attributable to specific AIFs, including an explanation of how the attribution was done and general information on remuneration criteria.

The AIFMD defines specific requirements with regard to the balance sheet to be published as an integral part of the annual report. According to Article 104 of Commission Delegated Regulation 231/2013, assets are defined as the resources controlled by the AIF from which future economic benefits are expected to flow to the AIF, and liabilities are present obligations of the AIF, the settlement of which is expected to result in an outflow from the AIF. The net assets represent the residual interest in the assets of the AIF after deducting all its liabilities. The assets have to be classified by:

(i)   investments;

(ii)   cash and equivalents;

(iii)   receivables.

Liabilities must be classified into:

(i)   accounts payable;

(ii)   borrowings;

(iii)   other liabilities.

Further, the income and expenditure account must be structured in accordance with Article 104. Income is defined as any increase and expenses are defined as any decrease in economic benefits during the accounting period. The net income or expenditure represents the excess of income over expenditure or expenditure over income. The income side of the account has to be classified by:

(i)   investment income;

(ii)   realised gains on investments;

(iii)   unrealised gains on investments;

(iv)   other income.

The expenses side of the account must be classified by:

(i)   management fees;

(ii)   other expenses;

(iii)   realised loss on investments;

(iv)   unrealised loss on investments.

Article 105 of Commission Delegated Regulation 231/2013 sets the minimum standard with regard to the information on the AIF's activities. At a minimum, it is required to:

(i)   describe the investment activities;

(ii)   provide the investment portfolio of the AIF;

(iii)   review the investment performance;

(iv)   describe the AIF's principal risks;

(v)   provide information on investment and economic uncertainties;

(vi)   provide financial and non-financial key performance indicators.

The report on the activities of the financial year should be together with the financial statement of the AIF. The accounting information provided with the annual report must undergo an independent audit as defined in Directive 2006/43/EC (statutory audits of annual accounts and consolidated accounts). The auditor's report, including all qualifications, must be reproduced in full in the annual report.

11.2)   The prospectus:

Before investing in any AIF, the AIFM must disclose specific information to investors. This information can be clustered into five main categories:

(i)   general information;

(ii)   processes and procedures;

(iii)   investment strategy;

(iv)   contractual relationships;

(v)   other mandatory information.

The general information must contain:

(i)   details on where any master AIF (if applicable) and where the underlying funds are established (in case of a fund of funds construction);

(ii)   information on the jurisdiction and the applicable law;

(iii)   the identity and the duties of the AIFM, the AIF, the depositary, the auditor, and other service providers;

(iv)   the identity of the prime brokers and potential conflicts of interest with regard to the depositary.

Regarding the processes and procedures, the AIFM must provide information on:

(i)   the procedure by which the AIF can change its investment strategy and policy;

(ii)   the valuation policy and the pricing methodology;

(iii)   the liquidity risk management and the redemption rights under normal and exceptional circumstances;

(iv)   the current redemption arrangements with investors;

(v)   how the AIFM ensures fair treatment of investors;

(vi)   the procedures and conditions for the issuance or sale of new shares.

If it is foreseen that investors can receive preferential treatment, the AIFM must add a description of what the preferential treatment can be and when it can be applied. The information on the investment strategy must contain information on:

(i)   the investment strategy and the objectives;

(ii)   the type of assets in which the AIF is eligible to invest;

(iii)   the associated risks;

(iv)   the investment restrictions;

(v)   the situations in which the AIF can use leverage;

(vi)   the types of leverage permitted, including their associated risks;

(vii)   the maximum level of leverage which can be employed for the AIF;

(viii) the restrictions with regard to the use of leverage and any asset or collateral reuse.

If the AIFMD requires the AIFM to provide information on contractual relationships, which entails informing investors about all the tasks delegated to third parties, the AIFM must disclose to investors the identity of the delegate and how professional liabilities are covered. In addition, it must provide a description of all fees, charges and expenses.

Before investing, the AIFM must provide to investors:

(i)   information about any discharge of liability arrangements with the depositary;

(ii)   the latest annual report;

(iii)   the latest market price or net asset value of the AIF;

(iv)   the historic performance of the AIF.

11.3) Periodic disclosures to investors:

The AIFM must periodically disclose specific information to investors. The information should be provided as part of the AIF's periodic reporting to investors, as required by the AIF's instruments of incorporation, or at the same time as the prospectus and offering document and at the same time as the annual report is made available or made public. Consequently the AIFM must renew the information at least once a year and whenever it markets the AIF to investors. It must disclose:

(i)   the percentage of illiquid assets;

(ii)   how management and performance fees apply to those assets;

(iii)   any new arrangement for managing the liquidity of the AIF;

(iv)   changes that are made to the liquidity management system and procedures;

(v)   the current risk profile of the AIF, including information on the risk management system to manage the risk;

(vi)   measures to assess the sensitivity of the AIF's portfolio to the most relevant risks where re risk limits have been exceeded or are likely to be exceeded;

(vii)   the circumstances and remedial measures to bring the AIF back in line with those limits;

(viii) changes made to the risk management system;

(ix)   any changes to the maximum level of leverage or the reuse of collateral, whereby it is necessary to show the original and revised maximum level of leverage calculated in accordance with the gross and commitment method;

(x)   the total amount of leverage employed by a specific AIF;

(xi)   the nature of rights granted for the reuse of collateral;

(xii) the nature of guarantees granted;

(xiii) details of any service provider changes with regard to leverage, collateral and guarantees.

An immediate notification to investors is required whenever redemptions are suspended. Commission Delegated Regulation 231/2013 also stipulates in Article 108, §3b that the investors must immediately be informed when side pockets and gates are activated. Unfortunately neither the AIFMD nor Directive 231/2013 defines what a side pocket or a gate is, but it seems that the European legislators are of the opinion that investors must be informed about the activation of these.

11.4) Reporting to competent authorities:

The AIFMD requires AIFMs to provide Competent Authorities with data about their activities and the activities of the AIFs they manage. The AIFM must transmit, on a regular basis, information on markets and instruments, liquidity and leverage. The AIFMD and Commission Delegated Regulation 231/2013 state that the AIFM must provide:

(i)   the main instruments and markets of trading;

(ii)   the principle exposures, including concentrations;

(iii) the percentage of illiquid assets;

(iv)   any new arrangements for managing the liquidity of the AIFs;

(v)   the current AIF risk profile;

(vi)   the risk management system to manage market, credit, liquidity, counterparty and operational risk;

(vii)   the market risk profile of the AIFs' investments, including the expected return and volatility in normal market conditions;

(viii)   the liquidity risk profile of the AIFs' investments, including the redemption and financing terms;

(ix)   the main categories of assets the AIFs are invested in, including short and long values, turnover and performance;

(x)   the results of the stress tests conducted according to the AIFMD's Article 15, §3b and Article 16 / §1;

(xi)   the overall level of leverage employed by each AIF, including a breakdown between leverage from borrowing or derivatives;

(xii)   the reuse of the AIFs' assets;

(xiii)   the identity of the 5 largest sources of borrowing for each AIF, including the amounts received from each source.

For non-EU AIFMs, reporting obligations are limited to EU AIFs managed by them and to non-EU AIFs marketed in the Union. The Competent Authorities may request additional information. The Competent Authorities of the AIFM's HMS must be notified about the appointment of the external valuer. AIFMs managing leveraged AIFs whose AuMs in total exceed 100 million EUR, and AIFMs managing unleveraged AIFs whose AuMs in total exceed 500 million EUR must provide the reporting package on a semi-annual basis. A quarterly reporting frequency is required for AIFMs managing AIFs whose AuMs in total exceed 1 billion EUR and for AIFMs managing leveraged AIFs whose AuMs exceed 500 million EUR. AIFMs managing unleveraged AIFs investing in non-listed companies just need to report on an annual basis.

Competent Authorities can demand reporting on a more frequent basis.

12.0) AIFMD terms and definitions:

No.	Term	Regulation	Article
1	Internally managed AIF	AIFMD Direction 2011/61/EU - 08.06.2011	§ 20 / sentence 1

Depending on their legal form, it should be possible for AIFs to be either externally or internally managed. AIFs should be deemed internally managed when the management functions are performed by the governing body or any other internal resource of the AIF. Where the legal form of the AIF permits internal management and where the AIF's governing body chooses not to appoint an external AIFM, the AIF is also AIFM and should therefore comply with all requirements for AIFMs under this Directive and be authorised as such. An AIFM which is an internally managed AIF should however not be authorised as the external manager of other AIFs. An AIF should be deemed externally managed when an external legal person has been appointed as manager by or on behalf of the AIF, which through such appointment is responsible for managing the AIF.

No.	Term	Regulation	Article
2	Interests of investors	AIFMD Direction 2011/61/EU - 08.06.2011	§ 12

Unless specifically provided for otherwise, where this Directive refers to the interests of the investors of an AIF the investors' interests in their specific capacity as investors of the AIF, and not their individual interests, are envisaged.

No.	Term	Regulation	Article
3	Issuer	AIFMD Direction 2011/61/EU - 08.06.2011	Article 4 / § 1t

"Issuer" means an issuer within the meaning of point (d) of Article 2(1) of Directive 2004/109/EC where that issuer has its registered office in the Union, and where its shares are admitted to trading on a regulated market within the meaning of point (14) of Article 4(1) of Directive 2004/39/EC.

No.	Term	Regulation	Article
4	Legal representative	AIFMD Direction 2011/61/EU - 08.06.2011	Article 4 / § 1u

"Legal representative" means a natural person domiciled in the Union or a legal person with its registered office in the Union, and which, expressly designated by a non-EU AIFM, acts on behalf of such non-EU AIFM vis-à-vis the authorities, clients, bodies and counterparties to the non- EU AIFM in the Union with regard to the non-EU AIFM's obligations under this Directive.

No.	Term	Regulation	Article
5	Leverage	AIFMD Direction 2011/61/EU - 08.06.2011	Article 4 / § 1v

"Leverage" means any method by which the AIFM increases the exposure of an AIF it manages whether through borrowing of cash or securities, or leverage embedded in derivative positions or by any other means.

No.	Term	Regulation	Article
6	Managing AIFs	AIFMD Direction 2011/61/EU - 08.06.2011	Article 4 / § 1w

"Managing AIFs" means performing at least investment management functions referred to in point 1(a) or (b) of Annex I for one or more AIFs.

| 7 | Marketing | AIFMD Direction 2011/61/EU - 08.06.2011 | Article 4 / § 1x |

"Marketing" means a direct or indirect offering or placement at the initiative of the AIFM or on behalf of the AIFM of units or shares of an AIF it manages to or with investors domiciled or with a registered office in the Union.

| 8 | Master AIF | AIFMD Direction 2011/61/EU - 08.06.2011 | Article 4 / § 1y |

"Master AIF" means an AIF in which another AIF invests or has an exposure in accordance with point (m).

| 9 | Member state of reference | AIFMD Direction 2011/61/EU - 08.06.2011 | Article 4 / § 1z |

"Member State of reference" means the Member State determined in accordance with Article 37(4).

No.	Term	Regulation	Article
10	Non-EU AIF	AIFMD Direction 2011/61/EU - 08.06.2011	Article 4 / § 1aa

"Non-EU AIF" means an AIF which is not an EU AIF.

No.	Term	Regulation	Article
11	Non-EU-AIFM	AIFMD Direction 2011/61/EU - 08.06.2011	Article 4 / § 1ab

"Non-EU AIFM" means an AIFM which is not an EU AIFM.

No.	Term	Regulation	Article
12	Non-listed company	AIFMD Direction 2011/61/EU - 08.06.2011	Article 4 / § 1ac

"Non-listed company' means a company which has its registered office in the Union and the shares of which are not admitted to trading on a regulated market within the meaning of point (14) of Article 4(1) of Directive 2004/39/EC.

No.	Term	Regulation	Article
13	Own funds	AIFMD Direction 2011/61/EU - 08.06.2011	Article 4 / § 1ad

"own funds" means own funds as referred to in Articles 56 to 67 of Directive 2006/48/EC.

No.	Term	Regulation	Article
14	Parent undertaking	AIFMD Direction 2011/61/EU - 08.06.2011	Article 4 / § 1ae

"Parent undertaking" means a parent undertaking within the meaning of Articles 1 and 2 of Directive 83/349/EEC.

No.	Term	Regulation	Article
15	Prime broker	AIFMD Direction 2011/61/EU - 08.06.2011	Article 4 / § 1af

"Prime Broker" means a credit institution, a regulated investment firm or another entity subject to prudential regulation and ongoing supervision, offering services to professional investors primarily to finance or execute transactions in financial instruments as counterparty and which may also provide other services such as clearing and settlement of trades, custodial services, securities lending, customised technology and operational support facilities.

No.	Term	Regulation	Article
16	Professional investor	AIFMD Direction 2011/61/EU - 08.06.2011	Article 4 / § 1ag

"Professional investor" means an investor which is considered to be a professional client or may, on request, be treated as a professional client within the meaning of Annex II to Directive 2004/39/EC.

No.	Term	Regulation	Article
17	Qualifying holding	AIFMD Direction 2011/61/EU - 08.06.2011	Article 4 / § 1ah

"Qualifying holding" means a direct or indirect holding in an AIFM which represents 10 % or more of the capital or of the voting rights, in accordance with Articles 9 and 10 of Directive 2004/109/EC, taking into account the conditions regarding aggregation of the holding laid down in Article 12(4) and (5) thereof, or which makes it possible to exercise a significant influence over the management of the AIFM in which that holding subsists.

No.	Term	Regulation	Article
18	Employee representatives	AIFMD Direction 2011/61/EU - 08.06.2011	Article 4 / § 1ai

"Employees representatives" means employees representatives as defined in point (e) of Article 2 of Directive 2002/14/EC.

No.	Term	Regulation	Article
19	Retail investor	AIFMD Direction 2011/61/EU - 08.06.2011	Article 4 / § 1aj

"Retail investor" means an investor who is not a professional investor.

No.	Term	Regulation	Article
20	Subsidiary	AIFMD Direction 2011/61/EU - 08.06.2011	Article 4 / § 1ak

"Subsidiary" means a subsidiary undertaking as defined in Articles 1 and 2 of Directive 83/349/EEC.

No.	Term	Regulation	Article
21	Supervisory author-ities in relation to Non-EU-AIFs	AIFMD Direction 2011/61/EU - 08.06.2011	Article 4 / § 1al

"Supervisory authorities" in relation to non-EU AIFs means the national authorities of a third country which are empow-ered by law or regulation to supervise AIFs.

No.	Term	Regulation	Article
22	Supervisory author-ities in relation to Non-EU-AIFMs	AIFMD Direction 2011/61/EU - 08.06.2011	Article 4 / § 1am

"Supervisory authorities" in relation to non-EU AIFMs means the national authorities of a third country which are empow-ered by law or regulation to supervise AIFMs.

No.	Term	Regulation	Article
23	Securitisations special purpose entities	AIFMD Direction 2011/61/EU - 08.06.2011	Article 4 / § 1an

"Securitisation special purpose entities" means entities whose sole purpose is to carry on a securitisation or securitisations within the meaning of Article 1(2) of Regulation (EC) No 24/2009 of the European Central Bank of 19 December 2008 concerning statistics on the assets and liabilities of financial vehicle corporations engaged in securitisation transactions (1) and other activities which are appropriate to accomplish that purpose.

No.	Term	Regulation	Article
24	UCITS	AIFMD Direction 2011/61/EU - 08.06.2011	Article 4 / § 1ao

"UCITS" means an undertaking for collective investment in transferable securities authorised in accordance with Article 5 of Directive 2009/65/EC.

No.	Term	Regulation	Article
25	AIF	AIFMD Direction 2011/61/EU - 08.06.2011	Article 4 / § 1a

For the purpose of this Directive, the following definitions shall apply: (a) "AIFs" means collective investment undertakings, including investment compartments thereof, which: (i) raise capital from a number of investors, with a view to investing it in accordance with a defined investment policy for the benefit of those investors; and (ii) do not require authorisation pursuant to Article 5 of Directive 2009/65/EC.

No.	Term	Regulation	Article
26	Branch of AIFM	AIFMD Direction 2011/61/EU - 08.06.2011	Article 4 / § 1c

"Branch" when relating to an AIFM means a place of business which is a part of an AIFM, which has no legal personality and which provides the services for which the AIFM has been authorised; all the places of business established in the same Member State by an AIFM with its registered office in another Member State or in a third country shall be regarded as a single branch.

No.	Term	Regulation	Article
27	Carried interest	AIFMD Direction 2011/61/EU - 08.06.2011	Article 4 / § 1d

"Carried interest" means a share in the profits of the AIF accrued to the AIFM as compensation for the management of the AIF and excluding any share in the profits of the AIF accrued to the AIFM as a return on any investment by the AIFM into the AIF.

No.	Term	Regulation	Article
28	Close link	AIFMD Direction 2011/61/EU - 08.06.2011	Article 4 / § 1e

"Close links" means a situation in which two or more natural or legal persons are linked by: (i) participation, namely ownership, directly or by way of control, of 20 % or more of the voting rights or capital of an undertaking; (ii) control, namely the relationship between a parent undertaking and a subsidiary, as referred to in Article 1 of the Seventh Council Directive 83/349/EEC of 13 June 1983 on consolidated accounts (1), or a similar relationship between a natural or legal person and an undertaking; for the purposes of this point a subsidiary undertaking of a subsidiary undertaking shall also be considered to be a subsidiary of the parent undertaking of those subsidiaries. A situation in which two or more natural or legal persons are permanently linked to the same person by a control relationship shall also be regarded as constituting a 'close link' between such persons.

No.	Term	Regulation	Article
29	Competent Authorities	AIFMD Direction 2011/61/EU - 08.06.2011	Article 4 / § 1f

"Competent authorities" means the national authorities of Member States which are empowered by law or regulation to supervise AIFMs.

No.	Term	Regulation	Article
30	Regulator in charge for the depositary	AIFMD Direction 2011/61/EU - 08.06.2011	Article 4 / § 1g

"Competent authorities" in relation to a depositary means: (i) if the depositary is a credit institution authorised under Directive 2006/48/EC, the competent authorities as defined in point (4) of Article 4 thereof; (ii) if the depositary is an investment firm authorised under Directive 2004/39/EC, the competent authorities as defined in point (22) of Article 4(1) thereof; (iii) if the depositary falls within a category of institution referred to in point (c) of the first subparagraph of Article 21(3) of this Directive, the national authorities of its home Member State which are empowered by law or regulation to supervise such categories of institution; (iv) if the depositary is an entity referred to in the third subparagraph of Article 21(3) of this Directive, the national authorities of the Member State in which that entity has its registered office and which are empowered by law or regulation to supervise such entity or the official body competent to register or supervise such entity pursuant to the rules of professional conduct applicable thereto; (v) if the depositary is appointed as depositary for a non- EU AIF in accordance with point (b) of Article 21(5) of this Directive and does not fall within the scope of points (i) to (iv) of this point, the relevant national authorities of the third country where the depositary has its registered office.

No.	Term	Regulation	Article
31	Competent Authority in charge for the AIF	AIFMD Direction 2011/61/EU - 08.06.2011	Article 4 / § 1h

"Competent authorities of the EU AIF" means the national authorities of a Member State which are empowered by law or regulation to supervise AIFs.

No.	Term	Regulation	Article
32	In control	AIFMD Direction 2011/61/EU - 08.06.2011	Article 4 / § 1i

"Control" means control as defined in Article 1 of Directive 83/349/EEC.

No.	Term	Regulation	Article
33	Established	AIFMD Direction 2011/61/EU - 08.06.2011	Article 4 / § 1j

"Established" means:(i) for AIFMs, 'having its registered office in'; (ii) for AIFs, 'being authorised or registered in', or, if the AIF is not authorised or registered, 'having its registered office in'; (iii) for depositaries, 'having its registered office or branch in'; (iv) for legal representatives that are legal persons, 'having its registered office or branch in'; (v) for legal representatives that are natural persons, 'domiciled in';

No.	Term	Regulation	Article
34	EU-AIF	AIFMD Direction 2011/61/EU - 08.06.2011	Article 4 / § 1k

"EU AIF" means: (i) an AIF which is authorised or registered in a Member State under the applicable national law; or (ii) an AIF which is not authorised or registered in a Member State, but has its registered office and/or head office in a Member State;

No.	Term	Regulation	Article
35	Feeder AIF	AIFMD Direction 2011/61/EU - 08.06.2011	Article 4 / § 1m

"Feeder AIF" means an AIF which: (i) invests at least 85 % of its assets in units or shares of another AIF (the 'master AIF'); (ii) invests at least 85 % of its assets in more than one master AIFs where those master AIFs have identical investment strategies; or (iii) has otherwise an exposure of at least 85 % of its assets to such a master AIF.

No.	Term	Regulation	Article
36	Financial instru-ment	AIFMD Direction 2011/61/EU - 08.06.2011	Article 4 / § 1n

"Financial instrument" means an instrument as specified in Section C of Annex I to Directive 2004/39/EC;

No.	Term	Regulation	Article
37	Holding company	AIFMD Direction 2011/61/EU - 08.06.2011	Article 4 / § 1o

"Holding company" means a company with shareholdings in one or more other companies, the commercial purpose of which is to carry out a business strategy or strategies through its subsidiaries, associated companies or participations in order to contribute to their long-term value, and which is either a company: (i) operating on its own account and whose shares are admitted to trading on a regulated market in the Union; or (ii) not established for the main purpose of generating returns for its investors by means of divestment of its subsidiaries or associated companies, as evidenced in its annual report or other official documents;

No.	Term	Regulation	Article
38	AIF home member state	AIFMD Direction 2011/61/EU - 08.06.2011	Article 4 / § 1p

"Home Member State of the AIF" means: (i) the Member State in which the AIF is authorised or registered under applicable national law, or in case of multiple authorisations or registrations, the Member State in which the AIF has been authorised or registered for the first time; or (ii) if the AIF is neither authorised nor registered in a Member State, the Member State in which the AIF has its registered office and/or head office;

No.	Term	Regulation	Article
39	AIFM host member state	AIFMD Direction 2011/61/EU - 08.06.2011	Article 4 / § 1r

"Host Member State of the AIFM" means any of the following: (i) a Member State, other than the home Member State, in which an EU AIFM manages EU AIFs; (ii) a Member State, other than the home Member State, in which an EU AIFM markets units or shares of an EU AIF; (iii) a Member State, other than the home Member State, in which an EU AIFM markets units or shares of a non-EU AIF; (iv) a Member State, other than the Member State of reference, in which a non-EU AIFM manages EU AIFs; (v) a Member State, other than the Member State of reference, in which a non-EU AIFM markets units or shares of an EU AIF; or (vi) a Member State, other than the Member State of reference, in which a non-EU AIFM markets units or shares of a non-EU AIF.

No.	Term	Regulation	Article
40	Initial capital	AIFMD Direction 2011/61/EU - 08.06.2011	Article 4 / § 1s

"Initial capital" means funds as referred to in points (a) and (b) of the first paragraph of Article 57 of Directive 2006/48/EC.

No.	Term	Regulation	Article
41	Definition of the term capital commitment	Commission Delegated Regulation 231/2013 - 19.12.12	Article 1 / sentence 1

In addition to the definitions laid down in Article 2 of Directive 2011/61/EU, the following definitions apply for the purposes of this Regulation: (1) "capital commitment" means the contractual commitment of an investor to provide the alternative investment fund (AIF) with an agreed amount of investment on request by the AIFM.

No.	Term	Regulation	Article
42	Relevant person	Commission Delegated Regulation 231/2013 - 19.12.12	Article 1 / sentence 2

"Relevant person" in relation to an AIFM means any of the following: (a) a director, partner or equivalent, or manager of the AIFM; (b) an employee of the AIFM, or any other natural person whose services are placed at the disposal and under the control of the AIFM and who is involved in the provision of collective portfolio management services by the AIFM.

No.	Term	Regulation	Article
43	Definition of the terms securitisation, securitisation position, sponsor and tranche	Commission Delegated Regulation 231/2013 - 19.12.12	Article 50

For the purposes of this Section: (a) "securitisation" means a securitisation within the meaning of Article 4(36) of Directive 2006/48/EC; (b) 'securitisation position' means a securitisation position within the meaning of Article 4(40) of Directive 2006/48/EC; (c) 'sponsor' means a sponsor within the meaning of Article 4(42) of Directive 2006/48/EC; (d) 'tranche' means a tranche within the meaning of Article 4(39) of Directive 2006/48/EC.

No.	Term	Regulation	Article
44	Definition of loss of a financial instrument held in custody	Commission Delegated Regulation 231/2013 - 19.12.12	Article 100

Loss of a financial instrument held in custody 1. A loss of a financial instrument held in custody within the meaning of Article 21(12) of Directive 2011/61/EU shall be deemed to have taken place when, in relation to a financial instrument held in custody by the depositary or by a third party to whom the custody of financial instruments held in custody has been delegated, any of the following conditions is met: (a) a stated right of ownership of the AIF is demonstrated not to be valid because it either ceased to exist or never existed; (b) the AIF has been definitively deprived of its right of ownership over the financial instrument; (c) the AIF is definitively unable to directly or indirectly dispose of the financial instrument. 2. The ascertainment by the AIFM of the loss of a financial instrument shall follow a documented process readily available to the competent authorities. Once a loss is ascertained, it shall be notified immediately to investors in a durable medium. 3. A financial instrument held in custody shall not be deemed to be lost within the meaning of Article 21(12) of Directive 2011/61/EU where an AIF is definitively deprived of its right of ownership in respect of a particular instrument, but this instrument is substituted by or converted into another financial instrument or instruments. 4. In the event of insolvency of the third party to whom the custody of financial instruments held in custody has been delegated, the loss of a financial instrument held in custody shall be ascertained by the AIFM as soon as one of the conditions listed in paragraph 1 is met with certainty. There shall be certainty as to whether any of the conditions set out in paragraph 1 is fulfilled at the latest at the end of the insolvency proceedings. The AIFM and the depositary shall monitor closely the insolvency proceedings to determine whether all or some of the financial instruments entrusted to the third party to whom the custody of financial instruments has been delegated are effectively lost. 5. A loss of a financial instrument held in custody shall be ascertained irrespective of whether the conditions listed in paragraph 1 are the result of fraud, negligence or other intentional or non-intentional behaviour.

No.	Term	Regulation	Article
45	Depositary's discharge of liability in case of loss of a financial instrument	Commission Delegated Regulation 231/2013 - 19.12.12	Article 101

A depositary's liability under the second subparagraph of Article 21(12) of Directive 2011/61/EU shall not be triggered provided the depositary can prove that all the following conditions are met: (a) the event which led to the loss is not the result of any act or omission of the depositary or of a third party to whom the custody of financial instruments held in custody in accordance with point (a) of Article 21(8) of Directive 2011/61/EU has been delegated; (b) the depositary could not have reasonably prevented the occurrence of the event which led to the loss despite adopting all precautions incumbent on a diligent depositary as reflected in common industry practice; (c) despite rigorous and comprehensive due diligence, the depositary could not have prevented the loss. This condition may be deemed to be fulfilled when the depositary has ensured that the depositary and the third party to whom the custody of financial instruments held in custody in accordance with point (a) of Article 21(8) of Directive 2011/61/EU has been delegated have taken all of the following actions: (i) establishing, implementing, applying and maintaining structures and procedures and insuring expertise that are adequate and proportionate to the nature and complexity of the assets of the AIF in order to identify in a timely manner and monitor on an ongoing basis external events which may result in loss of a financial instrument held in custody; (ii) assessing on an ongoing basis whether any of the events identified under point (i) presents a significant risk of loss of a financial instrument held in custody;

(iii) informing the AIFM of the significant risks identified and taking appropriate actions, if any, to prevent or mitigate the loss of financial instruments held in custody, where actual or potential external events have been identified which are believed to present a significant risk of loss of a financial instrument held in custody. 2. The requirements referred to in points (a) and (b) of paragraph 1 may be deemed to be fulfilled in the following circumstances: (a) natural events beyond human control or influence; (b) the adoption of any law, decree, regulation, decision or order by any government or governmental body, including any court or tribunal, which impacts the financial instruments held in custody; (c) war, riots or other major upheavals. 3. The requirements referred to in points (a) and (b) of paragraph 1 shall not be deemed to be fulfilled in cases such as an accounting error, operational failure, fraud, failure to apply the segregation requirements at the level of the depositary or a third party to whom the custody of financial instruments held in custody in accordance with point (a) of Article 21(8) of Directive 2011/61/EU has been delegated. 4. This Article shall apply mutatis mutandis to the delegate when the depositary has contractually transferred its liability in accordance with Article 21(13) and (14) of Directive 2011/61/EU.

No.	Term	Regulation	Article
46	Objective reasons for the depositary to contract a discharge of liability	Commission Delegated Regulation 231/2013 - 19.12.12	Article 102

Objective reasons for the depositary to contract a discharge of liability 1. The objective reasons for contracting a discharge pursuant to Article 21(13) of Directive 2011/61/EU shall be: (a) limited to precise and concrete circumstances characterising a given activity; (b) consistent with the depositary's policies and decisions. 2. The objective reasons shall be established each time the depositary intends to discharge itself of liability. 3. The depositary shall be deemed to have objective reasons for contracting the discharge of its liability in accordance with Article 21(13) of Directive 2011/61/EU when the depositary can demonstrate that it had no other option but to delegate its custody duties to a third party. In particular, this shall be the case where: (a) the law of a third country requires that certain financial instruments be held in custody by a local entity and local entities exist that satisfy the delegation criteria laid down in Article 21(11) of Directive 2011/61/EU; or (b) the AIFM insists on maintaining an investment in a particular jurisdiction despite warnings by the depositary as to the increased risk this presents.

Biography of Heiko Timm

In 1991, Heiko started a practical training with a large global bank in Hamburg, Germany. After successfully finishing the training and spending some time in the industry, he volunteered for military service in the German Navy, joining two missions in the Mediterranean Sea in 1995. In 2000 he received a law degree in banking and insurance law and signed up with UBS in Frankfurt, Germany. As chief of staff for products & services, he was responsible for implementing portfolio management and client reporting systems. In 2004 he became the head of the quality assurance department and he redesigned the asset management and investment guidelines monitoring processes of UBS Deutschland AG. In 2006, UBS AG, Zürich offered him the deputy head position of a large IT unit that developed and maintained most of UBS's portfolio management and advisory tools and systems. In 2009, already equipped with some valuable business experience, Heiko joined the Risk Effectiveness Program, a large scale risk remediation programme for recalibrating UBS's risk profile. From 2011 to the end of 2014 he worked in the Operational Risk Control and Compliance department of UBS Global Asset Management, being responsible for International Fund Services and the Swiss market. He specialised in Product Risk, Business Conduct Risk and Outsourcing and Offshoring-related risk; in addition, he developed models and methodology for integrating regulatory change and new financial market regulation in the Operational Risk and Compliance control framework.

In 2013 he earned the Six Sigma Black Belt degree. In December 2014 Heiko left UBS and currently holds the position of Chief Operating Officer at ACOLIN Fund Services AG, Zürich, Switzerland.